Water and Carbon Cycles

Geography AQA A-Level and AS Level (2016+) Study Guide

C McDonnell

I would like to give personal thanks to...

My family, for all the support you have given to help make this happen.

SW, for your outstanding copy editing skills. You're a star.

Thank you.

ISBN-13: 978-1535571968
ISBN-10: 1535571969

contents

3.1.1.1 Water and carbon cycles as natural systems
Systems in physical geography: **systems concepts** and their application to the water and carbon cycles inputs – outputs, energy, stores/components, flows/transfers, positive/negative feedback, dynamic equilibrium.

3.1.1.2 The water cycle
Global distribution and size of major stores of water – lithosphere, hydrosphere, cryosphere and atmosphere.

3.1.1.2 The water cycle
Processes driving change in the magnitude of these stores over time and space, including flows and transfers: evaporation, condensation, cloud formation, causes of precipitation and cryospheric processes at hill slope, drainage basin and global scales with reference to varying timescales involved.

3.1.1.2 The water cycle
Drainage basins as open systems – inputs and outputs, to include precipitation, evapotranspiration and run-off; stores and flows, to include interception, surface, soil water, groundwater and channel storage; stemflow, infiltration, overland flow and channel flow. Concept of water balance.

contents

contents

About this book

This student guide has been written to help support you through the key theoretical content, linked to the physical Geography topic 'water and carbon cycles' for the new (2016+) AQA A-level and AS level.

Through-out you will notice '**specification links**'; these are lifted directly from the AQA exam specification, and outline what they expect students' to know for the exams.

Key content addressing this criteria is clearly shown under a bannered sub-title.

On each page you will find key geographical theory along with suggested **learning tasks**, **further reading** and **exam practice** that is designed to test and embed your knowledge.

Specification links

3.1.1.2 The water cycle
Drainage basins as open systems – inputs and outputs, to include precipitation, evapotranspiration and run-off; stores and flows, to include interception, surface, soil water, groundwater and channel storage; stemflow, infiltration, overland flow and channel flow. Concept of water balance.

What is a drainage basin?

Drainage basins are a component (sub-system) of the hydrological cycle, which are local, **open systems**. They are 'open' because there is a movement of water both into, and out of, the system.

A drainage basin can be defined as an area of land drained by a river and its **tributaries** (river system). Drainage basins are separated by a boundary called a **watershed**, which is usually a ridge of high land. Any water that enters into this **catchment area** feeds into the river system within that drainage basin.

The drainage basin as a system...

Precipitation — Evaporation — Stemflow — Interception (by vegetation) — Evapotranspiration — Overland flow (runoff) — Surface storage (lakes, ponds etc.) — Evaporation — Infiltration (into the soil) — Channel storage — Throughflow — Storage (Soil moisture) — Percolation (through rocks + soil) — Groundwater flow — Storage (Groundwater) — Channel flow

Input □
Store □
Flow/transfer □
Output □

YOUR LEARNING TASK:
Add definitions to the glossary for each of these terms.
Now, convert this systems diagram into a written narrative that describes and explains the movement of water through a drainage basin.

Interception can be defined as the capture of **precipitation** by the plant canopy. This water can be stored and then returned to the atmosphere through **evaporation**.

The amount of precipitation intercepted by plants varies with leaf type, canopy architecture, wind speed, temperature and the humidity in the atmosphere.

Vegetation can intercept up to 50% of the rain that falls on its leaves. Water dripping off leaves to the ground surface is technically called **leaf drip**.

...ow is the process that directs **precipitation** down plant stems and branches. The redirection of water by this process causes the ground around the plant to receive additional moisture.

...mount of stemflow is determined by leaf shape, and stem and branch architecture. In general, **deciduous** trees have more stemflow than **coniferous** vegetation.

Cryospheric processes...

The cryosphere, which includes seasonal snow, frozen ground, sea ice, glaciers, ice caps, and ice sheets, is one of Earth's five main systems.

The influence of the cryosphere and cryospheric processes on stores, transfers and flows within the water cycle is significant.

It is estimated that the cryosphere contains about 1.8% of all water on Earth but nearly 70% of the freshwater.

On both a global and local scale the balance of water stored, and the salinity of the oceans, can have far reaching consequences for both physical processes and human interaction with the environment.

Components of the Cryosphere

At a global scale...

The **albedo effect** is one of the most powerful drivers of the Earth's climate.

Snow and ice, being a white surface, causes energy from the sun to be reflected back into space. However, land and oceans being much darker in colour absorb heat energy much more effectively.

As a result, the coverage of ice and snow on the planet creates a **positive feedback mechanism**. This means that the cryosphere is particularly sensitive to climate change, which in turn has a cumulative effect, that magnifies changes in climate globally.

Data, collected from ice cores, prove the cryosphere has repeatedly varied in size. This includes very large, long-duration changes, such as the **glacial** and **interglacial** periods, as well as much smaller (though still important changes), such as the Medieval Warm Period and Little Ice Age through-out the last two millennia. These are all a result of **natural changes** in climate.

However, more recent shifts in the concentrations of **greenhouse gases** is causing our planet to warm, as a result the cryosphere is shrinking rapidly. This will have impacts on global systems such as **ocean currents**, which can be altered by changes in **salinity** and **density** of the water (*see pages 36-37*). It will also lead to a reduction in albedo (reflectivity) and increase absorption of heat into the oceans (causing **thermal expansion**) and land. As a consequence, it causes further melting, and resultant sea-level rise and flooding, as land based ice and melt water from glaciers enters river and oceans.

At a local scale...

The snow and ice accumulation, and the temperature of the ground, will influence storage and the flow of water in a drainage basin. At a local scale temperature is greatly influenced by altitude; as the height above sea level increases temperatures fall. This is called the **lapse rate**.

-6°C   -9.8°C   1000 m

Lapse rate

YOUR LEARNING TASK:
Create a **mind map** to explain how changes to the cryosphere influence the water cycle.

EXAM PRACTICE:

Explain the concept of **dynamic equilibrium** in relation to the **water cycle**.   [4 marks]

Further reading resources:

Ocean currents and the Gulf Stream;
https://www.youtube.com/watch?v=UuGrBhK2c7U
Climate change and the cryosphere;
http://sites.gsu.edu/geog1112/lab-8-recent-climate-variability-change-part-2-under-development/

This study guide explores the main geographical content for this unit (3.1.1.1 – 3.1.1.4).

However, does <u>not</u> include qualitative and quantitative skills (3.1.1.5) or the local case study exemplar required for 3.1.1.6.

specification links

3.1.1.1 Water and carbon cycles as natural systems
Systems in physical geography: **systems concepts** and their application to the water and carbon cycles inputs – outputs, energy, stores/components, flows/transfers, positive/negative feedback, dynamic equilibrium.

What is a 'systems concept'?

'**Systems theory**' views the world as a complex system of interconnected parts.

We scope a system by defining its **boundary**; this means choosing which entities are inside the system and which are outside – part of the environment.

We then make simplified representations (models) of the system in order to understand, predict or impact its future behaviour.

Within the **boundary** of a system we can find three kinds of properties:
Elements - are the kinds of parts (things or substances) that make up a system. These parts may be atoms, molecules, or larger bodies of matter like sand grains, rain drops, plants, animals, etc.
Attributes - are characteristics of the elements that may be perceived and measured. For example: quantity, size, color, volume, temperature, and mass.
Relationships - are the associations that occur between elements and attributes. These associations are based on cause and effect.

A system can be a process or collection of **processes** that transforms **inputs** into **outputs**.

Very simply, inputs are consumed or enter into a system and outputs are produced or exit a system.

The concept of inputs and outputs can be very broad. For example, an output of a passenger ship is the movement of people from departure to destination. However, in relation to this course you will be associating it to the movement and flow of **water** and **carbon** through the water and carbon cycles, and through the **sub-systems** within these, such as **drainage basins** and the **nutrient cycle**.

Types of systems...

There are three main types of system, but primarily for this course we are mainly concerned with **closed** and **open systems**. You will need to apply your understanding of these different types of systems to the carbon and water cycles and the processes, flows and transfers within them.

Open system: This is a system in which both **mass** and **energy** are allowed to transfer across system boundary. This means there will be a flow of matter, like water, as well as energy into or out of the system.

Isolated system: There is no interaction between the system and its surroundings, they are completely isolated with no exchange of energy or mass. Practically, these type of systems do not exist and so are only theoretical.

Closed system: There may be a flow of energy into or out of the system, like radiation from the Sun, but no matter moves across the system boundary. This is a system with a fixed mass, so it neither gains nor loses a substance, for example water.

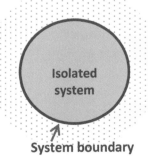

| YOUR LEARNING TASK: | Begin organising your study notes by adding to the **glossary**. For all the words in **bold** add a definition. Where necessary provide examples or diagrams to support each definition. |

Systems in context to Geography...

It is clear from the systems diagrams on the previous page, that our planet as a whole can be classified as a **closed system**.

Our planet is classed as a closed system and not an open or isolated system because...

The **carbon** and **water cycle** are systems that form relationships which allow energy, and mass, to transfer and flow between the different spheres of our planet.

As a **closed system** the water cycle has **no** overall input and output of mass.

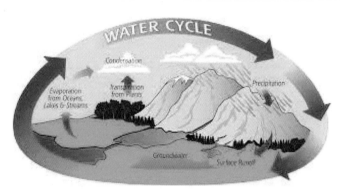

The water that was created on our planet when it was forming 4.5 billion years ago, plus water that was deposited by frequent comets in it's formative years, is the same water we have today.

The active water we use has, on average, been drunk 7 times before and was around when dinosaurs roamed our planet.

Figure 1:
Global distribution of the world's water

The **hydrological cycle** provides a model for understanding the global 'plumbing system' that links the atmosphere, oceans and land as it **evaporates**, **precipitates** and **flows**.

Water will spend time in the ocean, in the air, on the surface, and under the surface as **groundwater**.

It can exist as a solid, liquid and gas that are **interchangeable** according to the different temperatures found on Earth.

The **residence time** of water in each part of the hydrological cycle determines its impact on climates.

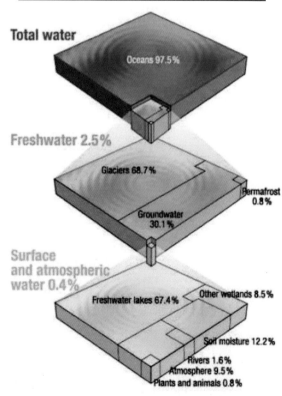

Source: Data from Shiklomanov and Rodda, 2003. Freshwater has a global volume of 35.2 million cubic kilometres (km³).

Cryosphere - The planet's frozen areas.

The **short time** spent by water in transit through the atmosphere results in short-term fluctuations in regional **weather** patterns.

Long residence times of 3,000 to 10,000 years in deep-ocean circulations, groundwater aquifers, and glacial ice act to moderate temperatures and **climates**.
These slower parts of the water cycle work as a system memory, which both store and release heat, buffering climate change.

Understanding key terms linked to the systems...

Within the water cycle (in **sub-systems**, like **drainage basins**) there are typical **OPEN SYSTEM** processes.

Inputs are the *things* (elements) that enter into a system.

Processes are actions and movements within the system. It is a general term that can also include **flows** and **transfers**

Process

Input

Output

Outputs are the ways in which the things (elements) in the system may leave the system boundary.

Feedback

A **feedback mechanism** is a process that uses the conditions of one component to regulate the function of the other. It is done to either increase or dampen the change in the system.

When the process tends to <u>increase change</u> in the system the mechanism is known as **positive feedback**.

Negative feedback is when the process seeks <u>to counter the change and maintain</u> **equilibrium**.

For example...

In a **drainage basin** if the **input** increases but the **output** does not then the size of storage will increase. This is an example of a **positive feedback**.

More carbon dioxide and an increase in temperature may, in general, result in more plant growth. This in turn increases photosynthesis which reduces CO_2, therefore leads to a **negative feedback**.

DYNAMIC EQUILIBRIUM...
The balanced state of a system when its inputs and outputs are equal.
If one element changes, because of some outside influence, this upsets the internal equilibrium and affects other components of the system. By a process of feedback, the system adjusts to the change and regains equilibrium.

Applying the basic systems concept to the water cycle...

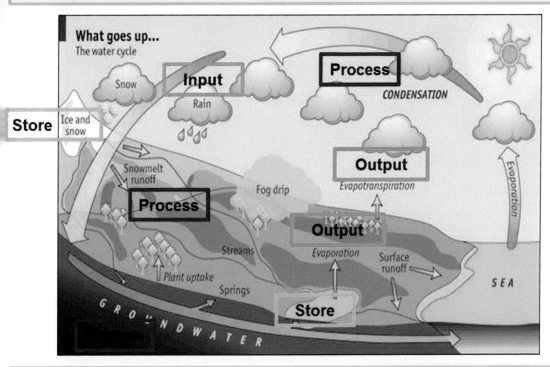

This diagram introduces the basic ideas of the system concept in a **drainage basin** (*see page 16*).

At A-Level you will need to demonstrate in-depth understanding of **inputs**, **processes** (flows and transfers) and **outputs** linked to drainage basins, and ultimately, the water cycle. These ideas are explored in more detail on pages 16 and 18.

YOUR LEARNING TASK:

Recap basic knowledge of the water cycle by explaining why these elements are classified as either an **input, process, store** or **output**.
For example: *Precipitation is an input because...*

specification links

Global distribution and size of major stores of water – lithosphere, hydrosphere, cryosphere and atmosphere.

What are the different spheres?

The **hydrosphere** refers to the water on the planet, whether it be on the surface, underground or in the air.

The **Cryosphere** is the frozen element of the hydrosphere. The quantity and location of water stored as ice will influence rates of reflectivity (**albedo**), water supplies and can be directly linked to climate and ocean currents.

©Andy Mahoney

The **atmosphere** is the blanket of gases that surround our planet. Air temperatures, currents, and moisture contents are key influential aspects of this sphere.

These key Earth systems demonstrate the unique properties of water and it's ability to exist in a variety of forms such a solid, liquid and a gas.

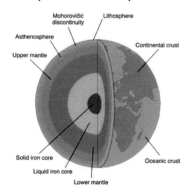

The **lithosphere** is the solid outer crust and upper portion of the Earth's mantle. This sphere is influenced by the hydrosphere and biosphere, which links to the **carbon cycle**.

The **biosphere** is part of the planet on which life dwells, from the deepest oceans, to the life abundant lithosphere and up to 6 km into the atmosphere.

In the solid state, the particles of matter are usually much closer together than they are in the liquid state. So if you put a solid into its liquid form, it sinks. But this is not true of water. Its solid state is less dense than its liquid state, so it floats.

Water is sometimes called the 'universal solvent' because it can dissolve so many things. This plays an important role when connecting the **water cycle** to the **carbon cycle**.

Water can absorb a large amount of heat, which allows large bodies of water to help moderate the temperature on Earth.

Further reading resources on the major earth systems;

https://nsidc.org/cryosphere/allaboutcryosphere.html

https://eo.ucar.edu/kids/green/cycles1.htm

http://nationalgeographic.org/encyclopedia/

Further reading resources on the properties of water and it's distribution:

http://www.dummies.com/how-to/content/the-unusual-properties-of-water-molecules.html

http://water.usgs.gov/edu/earthwherewater.html

Reading for the curious!

https://www.newscientist.com/article/dn25723-massive-ocean-discovered-towards-earths-core/

YOUR LEARNING TASK:	Using the information above and your own additional reading; Outline the ways in which the spheres interact with each other. Make specific reference to the movement of water and include as much specialist geographical vocabulary as possible.

Size and distribution of major water stores...

Figure 2:

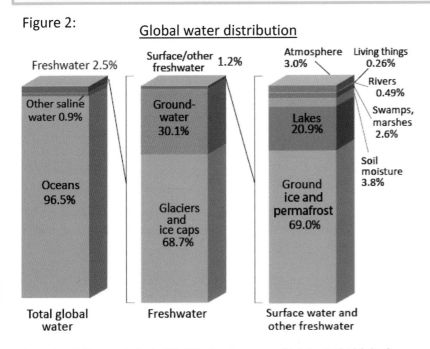

Global water distribution

Source: Igor Shiklomanov's chapter "World fresh water resources" in Peter H. Gleick (editor), 1993, Water in Crisis: A Guide to the World's Fresh Water Resources.
NOTE: Numbers are rounded, so percent summations may not add to 100.

To fulfil the specification requirements, you need to be able to describe the size and distribution of major stores of water in the spheres.

YOUR LEARNING TASK:

Using the information from figure 2 and the table 1, combined with your own research;

Write a summary to describe the size and distribution of water in the 4 different spheres.

Add depth and detail to your summaries by including key facts and information about each of the different spheres.
(*See further reading links on the previous page*).

Table 1:

One estimate of global water distribution
(Percents are rounded, so will not add to 100)

Water source	Water volume, in cubic miles	Water volume, in cubic kilometers	Percent of freshwater	Percent of total water
Oceans, Seas, & Bays	321,000,000	1,338,000,000	--	96.5
Ice caps, Glaciers, & Permanent Snow	5,773,000	24,064,000	68.7	1.74
Ground water	5,614,000	23,400,000	--	1.69
Fresh	2,526,000	10,530,000	30.1	0.76
Saline	3,088,000	12,870,000	--	0.93
Soil Moisture	3,959	16,500	0.05	0.001
Ground Ice & Permafrost	71,970	300,000	0.86	0.022
Lakes	42,320	176,400	--	0.013
Fresh	21,830	91,000	0.26	0.007
Saline	20,490	85,400	--	0.006
Atmosphere	3,095	12,900	0.04	0.001
Swamp Water	2,752	11,470	0.03	0.0008
Rivers	509	2,120	0.006	0.0002
Biological Water	269	1,120	0.003	0.0001

Source: Igor Shiklomanov's chapter "World fresh water resources" in Peter H. Gleick (editor), 1993, Water in Crisis: A Guide to the World's Fresh Water Resources (Oxford University Press, New York).

specification links

Water in its changing states...

Source:http://www.bbc.co.uk/bitesize/standard/physics/energy_matters/heat_in_the_home/revision/3/

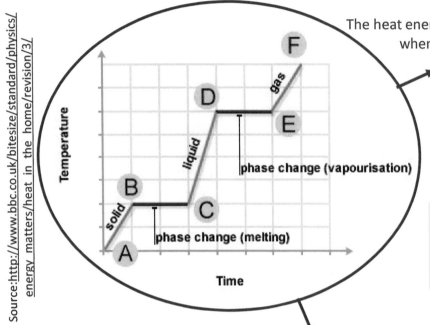

The heat energy that is taken in or given out by a substance when it changes state is called **latent heat**.

When a substance changes from solid to liquid, the latent heat involved is called the '**latent heat of fusion**'.

When the substance changes from a liquid to a vapour, it is '**latent heat of vaporisation**'.

You need to be able to explain these changes of state in relation to processes in the water cycle, and the associated timescales of each.

When heat energy is applied to a substance, or you remove heat from it, then you can cause the substance to change its state. Changes of state can be:
- **fusion**: the substance changes from a solid to a liquid
- **freezing**: the substance changes from a liquid to a solid
- **vaporisation**: the substance changes from a liquid into a vapour
- **condensation**: the substance changes from a vapour to a liquid

Gas

Solid ⟷ Liquid

When a substance is changing its state, **the temperature of the substance remains constant**. For example boiling water at 100 °C on changing state becomes steam (vapour) at 100 °C

Processes driving changes to stores over time and space...

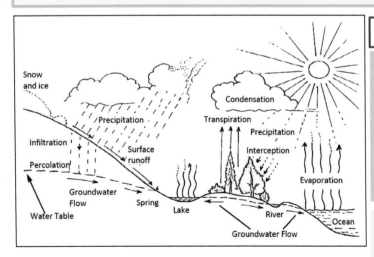

http://water.usgs.gov/edu/watercyclecondensation.html

YOUR LEARNING TASK:

Make or find a copy of the cycle diagram (*see left*) and using the information from 'Water and Carbon Cycling' by M Evans, pages 4 – 6 combined with your own research (*see links below*), annotate your cycle diagram with information relating to the key processes (flows/transfers) and stores. *Be sure to include evaporation + condensation.*

Further reading: 'Water and carbon cycling', M. Evans. https://www.rgs.org/NR/rdonlyres/6FDC37EC-9324-4CE7-8A96-86DFCA1EABB0/0/SCO_WaterandCarbonCycling.pdf

Evaporation, evapotranspiration and condensation...

Evaporation occurs when water is heated, causing it to change state from a liquid into a gas. This gas then rises into the atmosphere.

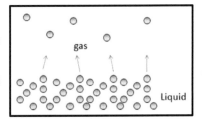

Evapotranspiration (often referred to as **transpiration**) is when water vapour is released, through the leaves of plants into the atmosphere.

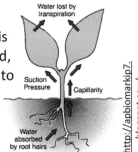

http://apbiomarkip7.blogspot.co.uk

The rates of **evaporation** and **evapotranspiration** can be influenced by many factors, but predominantly by **climatic factors** such as temperature, wind speeds and humidity. It is also influenced by **environmental factors** such as the vegetation type and the volume and area of surface water.

Condensation is simply the reversal of the evaporation process. As water vapour rises and cools it changes state back into a liquid.

High levels of evaporation and evapotranspiration will obviously reduce the amount of water stored as **surface water**, but also in **groundwater** as water is taken up by vegetation (*see page 19*). If rates of evaporation are high, it may suggest high temperatures, which could impact on water stored as ice and snow (*see page 15*).

However, as exemplified in tropical climates, this could lead to **convectional rainfall** (*see page 14*) which in turn could increase groundwater storage and surface water storage.

Cloud formation...

YOUR LEARNING TASK:

Below is a step-by-step guide to the formation of clouds.
Using this information convert these 6 points into a series of illustrations, to demonstrate cloud formation. For each point you could include key terms and/or a condensed summary of the process.

1. There is water around us all the time in the form of tiny gas particles, also known as **water vapour**. There are also tiny particles floating around in the air (such as salt and dust), these are called **aerosols**. The droplets are so small, with a diameter of about a hundredth of a millimetre. This means that each cubic metre of air could contain 100 million droplets.

2. The water vapour and the aerosols are constantly bumping into each other. When the air is cooled, some of the water vapour sticks to the aerosols when they collide—this is **condensation**.

3. Eventually, bigger water droplets form around the aerosol particles and these water droplets start sticking together with other droplets, forming **clouds**.

4. Clouds will either be composed of ice or water droplets, depending on the height of the cloud and the **temperature** of the **atmosphere**. Because the droplets are so small, they can remain in liquid form in temperatures as low as -30 °C. Extremely high clouds, at temperatures below -30 °C, are composed of ice crystals (cirrus clouds).

5. Clouds form when the air is **saturated** and cannot hold any more water vapour. The warmer the air is, the more water vapour it can hold. As the air rises it cools, reducing the temperature and therefore decreasing its ability to hold water vapour, so condensation occurs. The height at which **dew point** is reached and clouds form is called the **condensation level**.

6. As the tiny water droplets group together they grow heavy and **gravity** pulls them down as raindrops. If the air is cold enough, the ice crystals can remain frozen and grow large enough to fall as snow, sleet, freezing rain or hail.

Further reading resource: *http://www.metoffice.gov.uk/learning/clouds/what-are-clouds*

Causes of precipitation…

Convectional rainfall

The Sun's energy is concentrated in areas around the Equator, causing rapid, and high levels, of evaporation and evapotranspiration.

Large quantities of water vapour, combined with rapid condensation, creates heavy towering storm clouds such as cumulonimbus clouds.

Water vapour rises rapidly, causing condensation once **dew point** has been reached.

This is common in areas near the tropics, such as Brazil, Madagascar and Indonesia where they can experience heavy downpours during the afternoon.

This is common in places like the UK, where warm air from the tropics frequently mixes with cooler arctic and polar air masses.

Frontal rainfall

When the warm air meets cold, it is forced to rise. This is because it is lighter and less dense.

Along the 'front' a variety of different types of clouds form which can cause moderate to heavy rainfall.

However, as the warm air rises it begins to cool and as a result condenses to form clouds.

Orthographic rainfall

As the air rises, it cools and condenses. But because the cold air cannot hold as much moisture as warm air precipitation occurs.

Prevailing wind

As the air descends down the other side of the mountain it usually warms as it loses altitude, therefore it has a greater capacity to hold moisture. As a result so there is little rain on the far side of the mountain, creating an area called a **rain shadow.**

Moist warm air blown in across the ocean by the prevailing wind is forced to rise over areas of steep relief.

This is common along the west coast of the UK, Cumbria and the Lake District, due to the prevailing wind approaching from the west, laden with moisture from the Atlantic and Irish Sea.

Further reading resources:

Types of cloud!
http://www.bbc.co.uk/earth/story/20150716-nine-rare-and-beautiful-clouds

Interesting facts about rain…
http://www.metoffice.gov.uk/learning/rain/facts-about-rain

Types of rainfall;
http://www.metoffice.gov.uk/learning/rain/why-does-it-rain

http://www.curriculumbits.com/prodimages/details/geography/types-of-rainfall.html

YOUR LEARNING TASK:

Create a **flow diagram** for the 3 different types of rainfall.

EXAM PRACTICE:

Explain how evaporation affects stores of water in the spheres.

[4 marks]

Cryospheric processes...

The cryosphere, which includes seasonal snow, frozen ground, sea ice, glaciers, ice caps, and ice sheets, is one of Earth's five main systems.

The influence of the cryosphere and cryospheric processes on stores, transfers and flows within the water cycle is significant.

It is estimated that the cryosphere contains about 1.8% of all water on Earth but nearly 70% of the freshwater.

On both a global and local scale the balance of water stored, and the salinity of the oceans, can have far reaching consequences for both physical processes and human interaction with the environment.

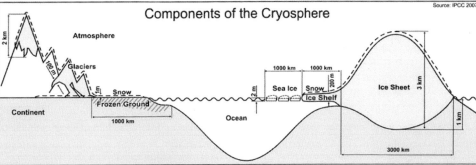

Components of the Cryosphere

Source: IPCC 2007

At a **global scale**...

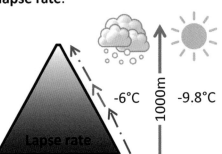

The albedo effect

The **albedo effect** is one of the most powerful drivers of the Earth's climate.

Snow and ice, being a white surface, causes energy from the sun to be reflected back into space. However, land and oceans being much darker in colour absorb heat energy much more effectively.

As a result, the coverage of ice and snow on the planet creates a **positive feedback mechanism**. This means that the cryosphere is particularly sensitive to climate change, which in turn has a cumulative effect, that magnifies changes in climate globally.

Data, collected from ice cores, prove the cryosphere has repeatedly varied in size. This includes very large, long-duration changes, such as the **glacial** and **interglacial periods**, as well as much smaller (though still important changes), such as the Medieval Warm Period and Little Ice Age through-out the last two millennia. These are all a result of **natural changes** in climate.

At a **local scale**...

The snow and ice accumulation, and the temperature of the ground, will influence storage and the flow of water in a drainage basin. At a local scale temperature is greatly influenced by altitude; as the height above sea level increases temperatures fall. This is called the **lapse rate**.

-6°C   1000m   -9.8°C

Lapse rate

However, more recent shifts in the concentrations of **greenhouse gases** is causing our planet to warm, as a result the cryosphere is shrinking rapidly. This will have impacts on global systems such as **ocean currents**, which can be altered by changes in **salinity** and **density** of the water (*see pages 36-37*). It will also lead to a reduction in **albedo** (reflectivity) and increase absorption of heat into the oceans (causing **thermal expansion**) and land. As a consequence, it causes further melting, and resultant sea-level rise and flooding, as land based ice and melt water from glaciers enters river and oceans.

YOUR LEARNING TASK:

Create a **mind map** to explain how changes to the cryosphere influence the water cycle.

EXAM PRACTICE:

Explain the concept of **dynamic equilibrium** in relation to the **water cycle**.   [4 marks]

Further reading resources:

Ocean currents and the Gulf Stream;
https://www.youtube.com/watch?v=UuGrBhK2c7U
Climate change and the cryosphere;
http://sites.gsu.edu/geog1112/lab-8-recent-climate-variability-change-part-2-under-development/

specification links

3.1.1.2 The water cycle

Drainage basins as open systems – inputs and outputs, to include precipitation, evapotranspiration and run-off; stores and flows, to include interception, surface, soil water, groundwater and channel storage; stemflow, infiltration, overland flow and channel flow. Concept of water balance.

What is a drainage basin?

Drainage basins are a component (sub-system) of the hydrological cycle, which are local, **open systems**. They are 'open' because there is a movement of water both into, and out of, the system.

A drainage basin can be defined as an area of land drained by a river

and its **tributaries** (river system). Drainage basins are separated by a boundary called a **watershed**, which is usually a ridge of high land. Any water that enters into this **catchment area** feeds into the river system within that drainage basin.

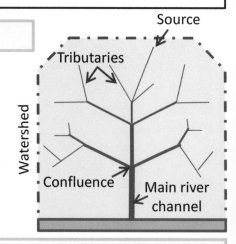

The drainage basin as a system...

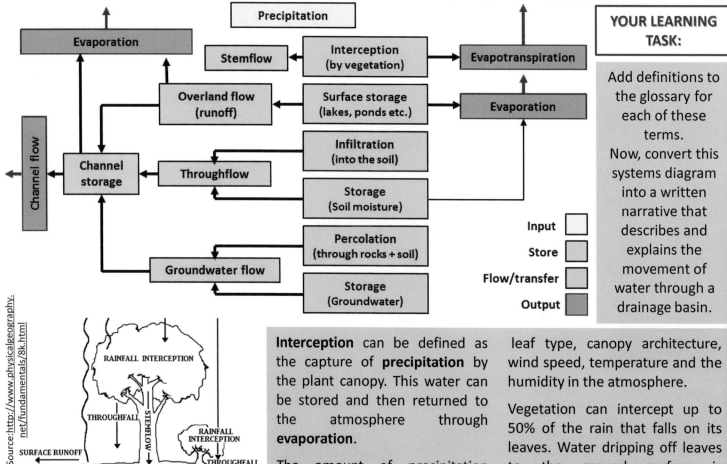

YOUR LEARNING TASK:

Add definitions to the glossary for each of these terms.
Now, convert this systems diagram into a written narrative that describes and explains the movement of water through a drainage basin.

Source: http://www.physicalgeography.net/fundamentals/8k.html

Interception can be defined as the capture of **precipitation** by the plant canopy. This water can be stored and then returned to the atmosphere through **evaporation**.

The amount of precipitation intercepted by plants varies with leaf type, canopy architecture, wind speed, temperature and the humidity in the atmosphere.

Vegetation can intercept up to 50% of the rain that falls on its leaves. Water dripping off leaves to the ground surface is technically called **leaf drip**.

Stemflow is the process that directs **precipitation** down plant stems and branches. The redirection of water by this process causes the ground around the plant to receive additional moisture.

The amount of stemflow is determined by leaf shape, and stem and branch architecture. In general, **deciduous** trees have more stemflow than **coniferous** vegetation.

The concept of water balance…

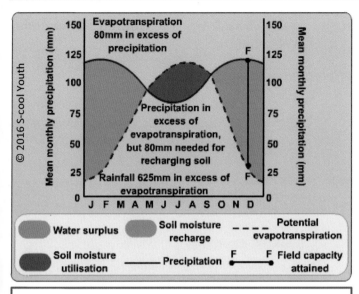

The balance between **inputs** and **outputs** is known as the **water balance** or budget.

The general water balance in the UK shows seasonal patterns of inputs and outputs. As shown (*left*), water balances and **river regimes** usually represent annual data; shorter term input, flows and outputs of water are presented in **flood hydrographs** (*see pages 18-19*).

During months where there are high rates of **precipitation** and little **evapotranspiration**, stores of water, for example in the soil, are 'recharged' and eventually generate a **water surplus**. Groundwater stores become **saturated**, which results in increased **surface runoff**, higher **discharge** and higher river levels. This means there is a positive water balance.

In drier seasons, evaporation and evapotranspiration exceed precipitation. During these dry months, stores of water are depleted, as a result there is a **water deficit** during the summer months.

Water balance can be shown using the formula:
**Precipitation (P) =
streamflow (Q) + evapotranspiration (E)
+/- changes in storage (S)**
P=Q+E +/- S

EXAM PRACTICE:

Using the **water balance** concept explain the how a **water deficit** can occur.   [4 marks]

YOUR LEARNING TASK:

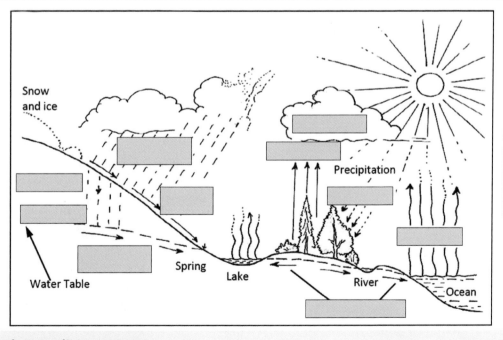

Copy out and fill in the blanks…without cheating!

Using the key terms explain **dynamic equilibrium** and link this to the **water balance**.

Further reading resources:

Drainage basins:
http://www.bbc.co.uk/scotland/education/int/geog/rivers/flash.shtml
http://www.alevelgeography.com/drainage-basin-hydrological-system/

Water balance graphs:
http://www.earthonlinemedia.com/ebooks/tpe_3e/hydrosphere/soil_moisture_seasons.html

specification links

Hydrographs can be used to illustrate how the **discharge** of a river changes as a result of **precipitation**. They cover a relatively short time period, usually hours or days rather than weeks or months.

This is the volume of water flowing through the river channel.

The **lag time** is the time difference between **peak flow** (the greatest volume of water in the river channel) and **peak rainfall**.

When precipitation first starts there is little increase in discharge. This is because little rain falls directly into the channel, but is being **intercepted** by vegetation, and **infiltrated** into the ground.

River Discharge		
=	cross sectional area	X rivers mean velocity

The hydrograph encompasses not just a line graph to show the **river discharge**, but also a histogram. This represents the amount of **precipitation** entering the drainage basin over time.

Bankfull discharge is the maximum discharge that a particular river channel is capable of carrying without flooding

Rates of water movement via **through flow** are usually low. Rates of maximum flow occur on steep slopes and in **pervious** sediments.

The lowest rates of flow occur in soils such as heavy clays. Rates of through flow in these sediments can be less than 1 millimetre per day.

Base flow represents the normal day to day discharge of the river and is the consequence of groundwater seeping into the river channel.

Falling limb (recession/receding limb) is how long it takes for river discharge to reduce. This may be slower because of **through flow** and groundwater flow which feeds the river at a slower rate.

Groundwater moves relatively slowly, ranging from several feet per day to just a few feet per year. As a result the age of groundwater (length of time spent in the subsurface) ranges from decades to millennia.

Factors influencing runoff and the flood hydrograph...

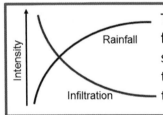

The **type and duration of precipitation** is an important factor to consider in relation to **runoff** variation. As shown in the figure (*left*) high intensity rainfall can lead to rapid runoff because the water cannot **infiltrate** into the ground quickly enough.

Drizzle, of course, is fine, close together drops smaller than 0.5mm in diameter that precipitate less than 1mm per hour.

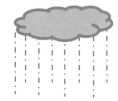

Rain is classified as drops with a diameter larger than 0.5mm which are widely separated.

Heavy rain can precipitate around 8mm per hour. Obviously torrential rain can result in large quantities being deposited. The record in USA is 305mm in 1 hour!

Factors influencing runoff and the flood hydrograph…

The amount of water and time taken to enter into the river channel can be influenced by a wide range of human and physical factors. You may need to interpret, explain and compare **flood hydrographs** in different locations therefore it is important to have a good understanding of these influential factors.

LAND USE

The amount, the type of **vegetation,** and even the season, influences the amount of rain **intercepted**. Verdant and leafy vegetation with large canopy surface areas will result in more interception (and stemflow). As a result it takes longer, and there will be less water, reaching, infiltrating and travelling as throughflow (and groundwater) into the river.

Urbanisation – The built environment has significantly more concrete and tarmac (**impermeable surfaces**). Therefore there is **little**, or **no infiltration**, leading to **rapid runoff** which means the **peak flow** is achieved quickly, with a short **lag time**. This is aided by the channelling of precipitation through guttering and drainage systems, such as storm sewers, which are efficient ways of directing water into the river channel.

Graph to show the soil moisture budget/water balance.

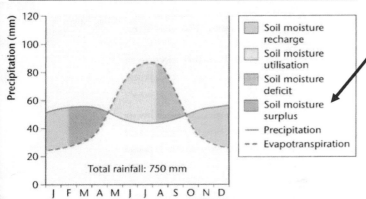

SOIL MOISTURE

Saturated soil has absorbed as much water as it can, therefore anymore water will simply **runoff** and transfer as **overland flow**, which is the quickest means by which water can reach and enter the river channel. For more in-depth explanation of the water budget, also known as the **soil moisture budget** (*see page 17*).

CLIMATE

Extremes in weather impact the rate and flow of water into the river channel. For example, in **winter** frozen ground becomes impermeable, or precipitation falls as snow or forms ice, which is stored. These can create **longer lag times** which may have a more **gradual discharge** into the river; unless there is sudden melting and **rapid influx** of melt water, especially if the ground is still frozen. In **summer** the ground can bake hard making it difficult for the water to **infiltrate** into the ground. When combined with the increased likelihood of heavy convectional rainfall, this can lead to rapid runoff and possibly flash flooding.

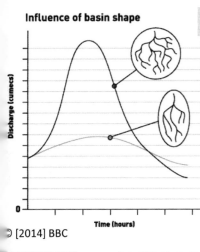

DRAINAGE BASIN

The **size** of the drainage basin will influence the **catchment area**. Simply put, if it has a large catchment and drainage area, with lots of tributaries, then it will have a greater volume of water entering the main river channel. The shape of the drainage basin will also affect the length of time it takes for the water to travel through the drainage basin, to reach the main channel.

SHAPE OF THE LAND

The **relief** in a catchment area will also influence the speed at which water travels into the main river channel, as shown in the graph (*right*).

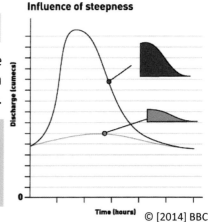

© [2014] BBC

YOUR LEARNING TASK:

Using the link below, test your knowledge and understanding of drainage basins and hydrographs by completing the questions.
http://www.bbc.co.uk/scotland/education/int/geog/rivers/questions/index.shtml

specification links

3.1.1.2 The water cycle

3.1.1.2 The water cycle
Changes in the water cycle over time to include natural variation including storm events, seasonal changes and **human impact including farming practices, land use changes and water abstraction**.

The water cycle as a system can easily be influenced by natural and human changes. These can modify and influence inputs, flows /transfers, and outputs of the water cycle system at global, national and regional/local scales. These changes inevitably alter the water balance, and can therefore disrupt the **dynamic equilibrium** to create **feedback** which can be positive and negative. Many of the natural changes, and some human impacts, have already been explored through the explanation of factors affecting flood hydrographs (*see pages 18 – 19*).

Human impacts on the water cycle...

As the population of the planet has increased, so has our demand for food, adding pressure to make land as productive as possible. The main outcomes of this increased productivity are changing farming practices, such as the use of irrigation systems and the application of chemicals such as fertilisers and pesticides. In addition to this people are accessing and utilising land which was previously unsuitable for farming, this may include previously arid or forested areas for example.

© 2016 Salamander Publishing.

Irrigation: This involves the **abstraction** and re-direction of water, from its natural course, to be applied to land so that crops have sufficient water to grow. The climate and the types of crop grown will influence how much water is required. **Drip irrigation** is a very effective and efficient way of watering crops, however many **spray irrigation** systems are much less efficient and can require large quantities of water. Without proper management, problems arise such as **over-abstraction** (taking too much water out) with possible resultant **salinisation** (increased salt content), as water is pumped from groundwater sources. Application of too much water can cause **leaching** of nutrients and applied chemicals, which causes increased run-off and **contamination** of water sources, which can lead to other problems such as **eutrophication** and **siltation**.

Land-use changes: As discussed on page 19, the amount and type of vegetation and urbanisation can have a significant impact on the **flood hydrograph**, and therefore the movement of water through the system. Other changes in land-use can also include **deforestation**,

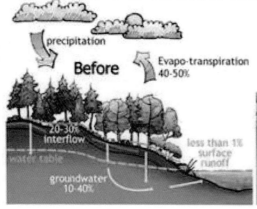
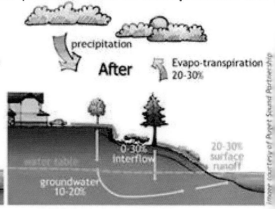

which can have a tremendous impact, not only on the movement of water, but also on **terrestrial carbon cycling** (*see pages 30 - 31*). The most significant impacts on the water cycle are shown on the graphic above, which illustrates how the removal of vegetation can impact local climates and rates of precipitation, as well as the movement of water through the drainage basin. Higher rates of **run-off**, as with **irrigation**, means **erosion** and **leaching** will also increase; inevitably degrading the quality of the land and water for future use.

Further reading resource: http://www.livescience.com/27692-deforestation.html

Using the information above, convert the text into either a series of illustrations or a flow diagram/mind map to show the consequences of these human activities on the water cycle.
Use the glossary and your own research to ensure accurate depictions of new terms are represented.

YOUR LEARNING TASK:

Human impacts on the water cycle continued...

Water abstraction: This is the removal of water, either permanently or temporarily, from rivers, lakes, canals, reservoirs or from underground strata (groundwater stores). This process is essential to meet the demands of growing populations and increased industrial and agricultural production. When too much water is removed then it is called **over-abstraction**. This is most likely to happen in areas that have high population densities and low levels of precipitation. Here water is being pumped out faster than it can be replenished, leading to a deficit that depletes the groundwater store.

The process of **over-abstraction** has led to falling **water tables**. As the level of water lowers it becomes increasingly difficult to extract, and it also influences the flow of rivers. As discussed in relation to hydrographs (*page 18*), **groundwater flow** is an important source to ensure that the **base flow** of a river is maintained. If the river is no longer being fed by this subterranean source, then during dry periods the river may no longer flow.

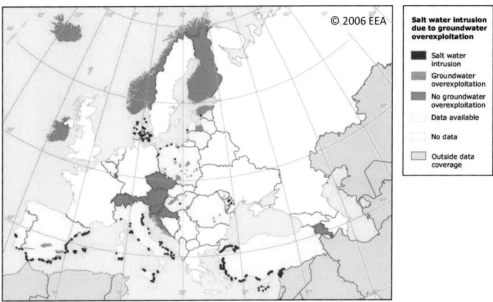

Over-abstraction can also lead to **salt-water intrusion** in **aquifers** near coastal areas. As shown on the map (*above*) this is a problem in many European countries.

YOUR LEARNING TASK:

Now that you have completed the main theory element on the water cycle note down the key words in bold. Write your own glossary or see if you can produce an extended piece of writing that includes and connects all of these key terms.

Further reading resources:

Overview:
https://www.youtube.com/watch?v=ci-ABWPG7LQ

River fieldwork techniques:
https://www.geography-fieldwork.org/rivers/river-variables/4-data-analysis.aspx
http://www.rgs.org/OurWork/Schools/Fieldwork+and+local+learning/Fieldwork+techniques/Rivers.htm

Flood hydrographs:
http://www.coolgeography.co.uk/GCSE/AQA/Water%20on%20the%20Land/Hydrographs/Hydrographs.htm
http://www.geography.learnontheinternet.co.uk/topics/discharge.html
http://www.s-cool.co.uk/a-level/geography/river-profiles/revise-it/storm-hydrographs-and-river-discharge

How the heaviest rainfall is happening in the UK:
http://news.bbc.co.uk/1/hi/8376031.stm

Human impacts on the water cycle:
https://www.youtube.com/watch?v=HOtQ_iRq4Tk
http://www.eea.europa.eu/themes/water/water-resources/impacts-due-to-over-abstraction

The water and carbon cycles are closed systems. What does this mean?

Explain how the systems concept applied to the water cycle.   [4 marks]

Outline how changes in the cryosphere can lead to positive feedback in the hydrosphere.   [4 marks]

Using the figure (*right*)...
Describe the distribution and size of the worlds major store of water. Making reference to the different spheres in which they are found.   [6 marks]

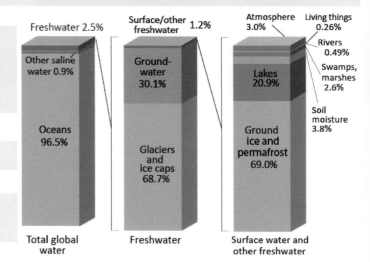

How are clouds formed?

Explain the differences between convectional , frontal and orthographic rainfall.

Compare and explain why discharge on these flood hydrographs is different despite receiving the same amount of precipitation.
A good quality answer should provide at least 4 reasons for the differences, and include a range of appropriate and specialist geographical terminology.

Flood hydrograph A:

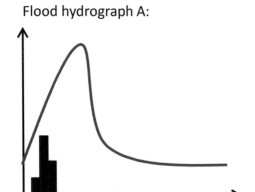

Flood hydrograph B:

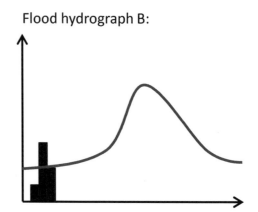

Explain the importance of ground water for both human and physical geography.

Assess the extent to which humans impact on the water cycle.   [20 marks]

Specification links

What is carbon and why is it important?

You may not realise, but carbon is the fourth most abundant element in the universe (after hydrogen, helium and oxygen) and it is essential to life on Earth. In fact, water and carbon combined makes up 83% of our bodies! In addition to ourselves, carbon is exceptionally diverse and can come in the form of a gas (CO_2) or more solidly from diamonds, limestone, graphite, wood and plastics, to name just a few.

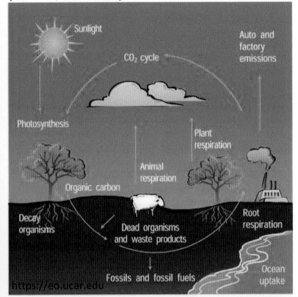

https://eo.ucar.edu

Like water the carbon cycle as a whole is a **closed system** which interacts with the different spheres on the Earth (*see page 5 + 8*).

It can be divided into '**living**' and '**non-living**' (*biogeochemical cycles*), also known as **biological** and **geological** components.

The 'living' or **organic** part of the carbon cycle can operate on a timescale of days up to thousands of years. The 'non-living' or **inorganic** component however, in the most part, relates to a much grander geological timescale of millions of years.

© 2013
OpenStax College

YOUR LEARNING TASK:

Recap prior learning by summarising each sphere in just 5 words.

Distribution and size of carbon stores in the spheres...

The main **stores** (also known as reservoirs) of carbon are found in living and dead organisms in the biosphere; as the gas **carbon dioxide** in the atmosphere; as organic matter in soils; as **fossil fuels** and **sedimentary rocks** (such as limestone and chalk) in the lithosphere; in the oceans as dissolved atmospheric carbon dioxide and in the shells (calcium carbonate) of marine organisms; and finally, vast quantities are stored in ice and permafrost (found in the Arctic) as methane and carbon dioxide.

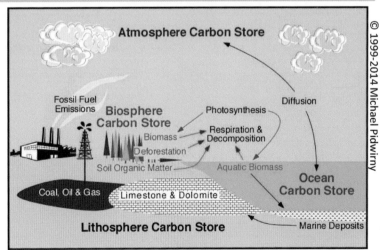

© 1999-2014 Michael Pidwirny

As shown in both carbon cycle diagrams (*above*), like water, carbon is transferred between the spheres.

YOUR LEARNING TASK:

Using all the information provided on this page describe the distribution and amount of carbon found in the different spheres of the planet.

Carbon sink	Amount in metric tons (billions)
Atmosphere	578 (in 1700) - 766 (in 1999)
Soil Organic Matter	1500 to 1600
Ocean	38,000 to 40,000
Marine Sediments and Sedimentary Rocks	66,000,000 to 100,000,000
Terrestrial Plants	540 to 610
Fossil Fuel Deposits	4000
Permafrost and ice	1,400

Carbon sink is anything that absorbs more **carbon** that it releases

specification links

The carbon cycle as a system...

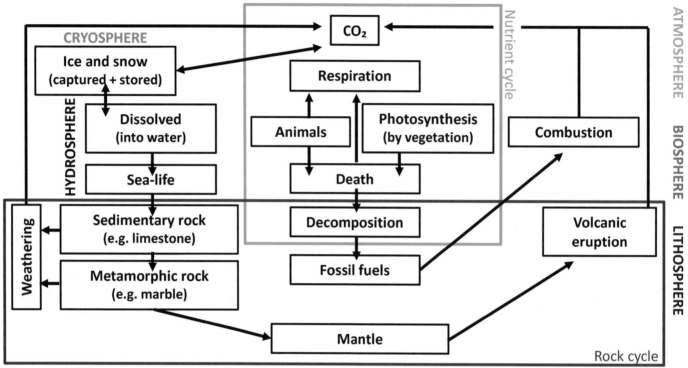

As illustrated in the systems diagram above the carbon cycle is a complex system that is essential to life. It includes a wide array of processes that transfer carbon between the spheres in a variety of different forms.

Flows and transfers between stores in the carbon cycle – Photosynthesis, respiration and decomposition

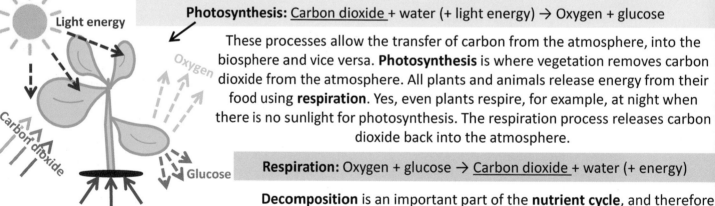

Photosynthesis: Carbon dioxide + water (+ light energy) → Oxygen + glucose

These processes allow the transfer of carbon from the atmosphere, into the biosphere and vice versa. **Photosynthesis** is where vegetation removes carbon dioxide from the atmosphere. All plants and animals release energy from their food using **respiration**. Yes, even plants respire, for example, at night when there is no sunlight for photosynthesis. The respiration process releases carbon dioxide back into the atmosphere.

Respiration: Oxygen + glucose → Carbon dioxide + water (+ energy)

Decomposition is an important part of the **nutrient cycle**, and therefore the carbon cycle as a whole. Most of the carbon absorbed or consumed is respired back into the atmosphere, but some is **stored**. For example, we already know that the human body is nearly 1/5th carbon. When vegetation and animals die, they are broken down (**decomposed**) and the nutrients within it are recycled back into the environment by 'decomposers', such as fungi and microbes. In doing this the decomposers release carbon dioxide through **respiration**.

In some conditions **decomposition** is blocked, for example when there is a lack of oxygen. When this happens plant and animal matter may be converted into fossil fuels which can be burnt to release energy and also carbon dioxide (*see page 25*).

Flows and transfers between stores in the carbon cycle – Combustion, weathering and carbon sequestration

Combustion is the burning of fuels which in turn generates heat and light. When this is considered in relation to the carbon cycle it can be presented as the equation;

Combustion: Hydrocarbon + oxygen → carbon dioxide + water

Hydrocarbons are a combination of hydrogen and carbon. We most commonly recognise these as derivatives from crude oil such as natural gas and petrol. However, anything that was once living contains hydrocarbons; hence why they burn. The consequence of combustion is explored on pages 27 – 28.

YOUR LEARNING TASK:

List all the key words in **bold** on the **carbon cycle** so far…
Add definitions in the glossary for each of these terms.
Include all these terms in a written piece that describes and explains the movement and storage of carbon between the spheres.

The **oceans** cover 71% of the Earth's surface and have an average depth of 3,800 metres. It is estimated, that the amount of **carbon stored in the oceans** is 50 x more than is contained in the atmosphere, and 20 x more than that found in plants and soil. As a result, the oceans provide a sizable and vitally important **carbon sink**, as the CO_2 is dissolved in the water. Over time the amount of CO_2 in the oceans has increased, generating a small changing the pH level in surface waters (*IPCC 2005*). Life in the oceans also absorbs some of the carbon (as calcium carbonate), eventually this will become part of the geological aspect of carbon sequestration as they become marine sediments.

Weathering is the gradual break down of rocks and can be categorised as **physical** (freeze-thaw and onion skin), **chemical** and **biological**. As rocks break down, the carbon stored within them is returned to the carbon cycle, either through the soil and the **nutrient cycle**, or through the movement of water through the **hydrological cycle**.
Carbon can be transported through the water cycle by chemical weathering, which happens when carbon dioxide from the atmosphere is combined with the hydrosphere; for example as rain, which is slightly acidic due to the CO_2.

©2009
Greg Carley.

This rain then 'weathers' the rocks using the weak acid. In this example the minerals released by the weathering process are washed into the sea where they become part of ocean **sequestration**.

Further reading resources:

Carbon cycle, stores and transfers;

http://www.visionlearning.com/en/library/Earth-Science/6/The-Carbon-Cycle/95

http://www.physicalgeography.net/fundamentals/9r.html

http://earthobservatory.nasa.gov/Features/CarbonCycle/page2.php

https://nsidc.org/cryosphere/frozenground/methane.html

Carbon sequestration in the oceans;

https://www.ipcc.ch/pdf/special-reports/srccs/srccs_chapter6.pdf

Weathering;

http://www.bbc.co.uk/bitesize/ks3/science/environment_earth_universe/rock_cycle/revision/6/

Carbon sequestration is the removal and storage of carbon from the atmosphere in **carbon sinks** (such as oceans, forests or soils). This occurs naturally through **geologic carbon sequestration**, where CO_2 is stored underground in rock formations (*see pages 23, 24 and 26*). Alternatively, it can be stored in plants and soil by **biological carbon sequestration**, through transfers such as photosynthesis and respiration which will vary according to ecosystem types (**seres**). For example tundra compared to tropical rainforest.

Carbon sequestration in **sediments** is where the largest quantity of carbon can be found (*see page 23*). Over millions, or even billions of years, processes linked to the **nutrient** and **rock cycle** (*see page 24*) mean that as living things have died they have been deposited on the ground. Over time stores of carbon have been compressed into rocks, or metamorphosed into other forms, such as fossil fuels like crude oil and coal.
As we extract reserves of fossil fuels from the ground, we are releasing ancient carbon back into the atmosphere.

EXAM PRACTICE:

Explain the role of **weathering** in the **carbon cycle**. [4 marks]

SPECIFICATION lINkS

3.1.1.3 The carbon cycle
Changes in the carbon cycle over time, to include natural variation (including wild fires, volcanic activity) and human impact (including hydrocarbon fuel extraction and burning, farming practices, deforestation, land use changes).

Natural causes of carbon variation...

The carbon cycle, like the water cycle, has a series of **subsystems** within it. One of these subsystems is the **rock cycle,** which connects the biosphere, atmosphere, *solar energy* hydrosphere and lithosphere.

As you can see (*right*) it is a complicated cycle that relates to materials and processes beyond carbon. However, for us to understand the **geological** component of the carbon cycle, it is essential to have an understanding of these processes. Carbon is transferred from the **biosphere** and **hydrosphere**, into the **lithosphere** as **sedimentary rock**, which is the largest store of carbon on the planet. Then back into the **atmosphere**, biosphere and hydrosphere through **weathering, burial, compaction, uplift** and **volcanic eruption**.

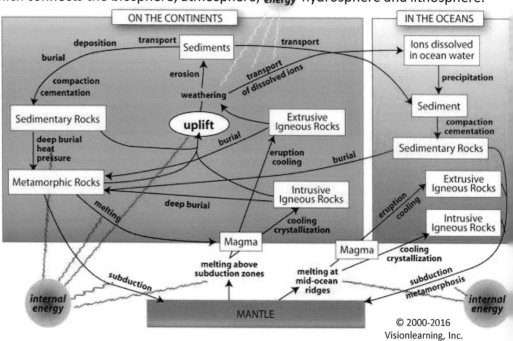

© 2000-2016 Visionlearning, Inc.

Volcanic activity: As you are no doubt aware, magma is a molten and semi-molten rock mixture found under the Earth's surface. Magma is made up of 4 different parts including dissolved gases; the most abundant being water vapour, carbon dioxide and sulphur dioxide. The amount of gas, combined with temperature and viscosity of the magma, are the driving forces behind volcanic eruptions. When volcanoes erupt, these gases can be released effusively and explosively into the atmosphere. For example, the large eruption of Mt Pinatubo in 1991 is estimated to have added more than 250 megatons of gas into the atmosphere in a single day. USGS monitoring of Kilauea have recorded discharges of CO_2 between 8,000 – 30,000 metric tonnes each day (USGS 2007). Volcanoes which fail to erupt can also release carbon dioxide, among other gases, into the atmosphere through the soil, volcanic vents and fumaroles.

Source: http://dilu.bol.ucla.edu/home.html

Storage in atmosphere (720 + 3/yr due to burning fossil fuels) *

Volcanoes (0.1/yr)

Burning fossil fuels (5 – 6/yr)

Land photosynthesis and respiration (120/yr)

Oceanic photosynthesis and respiration (107/yr)

Soil storage (1500) *

Coal

Oil

Storage in land plants (560) *

Weathering and erosion (0.6/yr)

Fossil fuel storage (4000) *

Storage in shallow and ocean waters 39,000 *

* Storage units in billions of metric tons of carbon
→ Indicates direction of carbon transfer in billions of metric tons/yr

Storage in marine sediments and sedimentary rocks (100,000,000)

Further reading resources:

https://volcanoes.usgs.gov/vhp/gas.html
www.bgs.ac.uk/downloads/start.cfm?id=432

Natural causes of carbon variation continued – Forest fires

As you should now be well aware, forests are a **carbon sink**. Through the process of photosynthesis trees absorb carbon dioxide. However, as they die and decay, or are consumed by **forest fire**, their carbon is released back into the air as carbon dioxide.

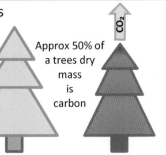

Approx 50% of a trees dry mass is carbon

'Every year, fires burn 3 million to 4 million square kilometres of Earth's land surface area, and release more than a billion tons of carbon into the atmosphere in the form of carbon dioxide.'
(MacMillan, 2007)

Forest fires can ignite new growth and rejuvenation in the forest, as nutrients are returned to the soil and saplings can spring forth, fuelled by sunlight. This sunlight that is able to reach the forest floor now that the previously dense canopy has been removed. The new vegetation reabsorbs much of the carbon dioxide that the fire had released, providing a natural balance. However, it is argued that large and more frequent fires, caused by human interaction and climate change, is impacting this delicate balance in a negative way.

Further reading resource:

Forest fires:
http://www.geotimes.org/nov07/article.html?id=WebExtra111207.html

Human impacts causing changes in the carbon cycle – Fuel extraction and burning

Hydrocarbons, also known as fossil fuels, are formed as pre-historic organic matter is **buried**. This organic matter is pressurised by the layers of earth above and heated from below.

Different types of organic material, and the level of pressure and heat that it is subjected to, influenced the type of fossil fuel created, such as coal, oil or gas.

Oil and natural gas are contained and prevented from rising and seeping out of the ground by 'caprocks', an impermeable layer of rock which traps the oil or gas below the surface. Extraction of oil and gas involves drilling through caprocks to capture and then pressure this **non-renewable, stock resource** from the lithosphere.

Further reading resource: http://www.fe.doe.gov/education/energylessons/coal/gen_howformed.html

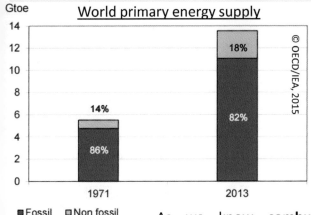

© OECD/IEA, 2015

Fossil fuels have a variety of different uses; they are found in medicines, make-up, any kind of plastic products and synthetic fabrics to name just a few. However, they are mainly used as a source of **energy**, which when **combusted** will power our vehicles, heat our homes and generate electricity.

Our demand for energy has increased dramatically over time as a result of **industrialisation**, and increasing standards of living. As shown in the graph (*left*) 82% of this energy is sources from fossil fuels.

As we know **combustion** produces carbon dioxide, however the amount produced depends upon the chemical make-up of the hydro-carbon being burnt.

For example, natural gas produces half the amount of CO_2 per unit to coal and oil, hence the comparatively low share in emissions.

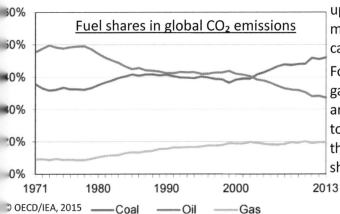

© OECD/IEA, 2015 —— Coal —— Oil —— Gas

Primary energy world consumption 2015
(million tonnes oil equivalent)

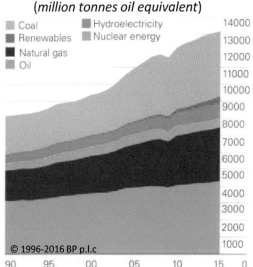

Coal, Renewables, Natural gas, Oil, Hydroelectricity, Nuclear energy

© 1996-2016 BP p.l.c

Human impacts causing changes in the carbon cycle – Fuel extraction and burning continued…

Once a hydrocarbon has been combusted it releases CO_2 as a gas back into the atmosphere, where it once again becomes part of the carbon cycle.

As human consumption of fossil fuels have increased, as has the amount of CO_2 in the atmosphere.

By using data from **ice cores** and other proxy data (such as micro fossils and sediments), scientists have ascertained that in the past 1 million years the amount of CO_2, measured in parts per million (ppm), has ranged from 170 – 300 ppm. Since the Industrial Revolution concentrations have increase beyond 300ppm and today they are recorded on and above 400ppm.

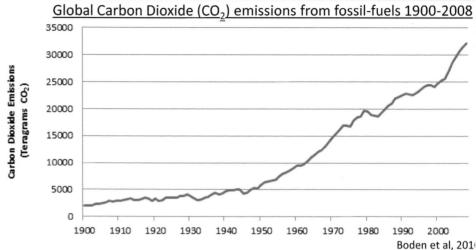

Global Carbon Dioxide (CO_2) emissions from fossil-fuels 1900-2008

Boden et al, 2010

YOUR LEARNING TASK:

Compare natural and human causes of variations in the carbon cycle to assess which has the largest impact.

Human caused release of carbon 2011:	
Gas hydrocarbons	1.7GT
Liquid hydrocarbons	3.317GT
Solid hydrocarbons	3.997GT
Other (e.g. cement production + gas flaring)	0.554GT
Total	9.568GT

Source: Oak Ridge National Laboratory, 2011.

Using this data, combined with our understanding of the carbon cycle as a system, it is clear that human activity is transferring carbon *from* stores into the atmosphere faster than the cycle can then move that carbon back *into* stores. Thus creating an imbalance that is affecting the **carbon budget** (*see page 33*).

Further reading resources:

http://www.bp.com/en/global/corporate/energy-economics/statistical-review-of-world-energy/primary-energy.html
http://www.iea.org/publications/freepublications/publication/co2-emissions-from-fuel-combustion-highlights-2015.html
https://www.co2.earth/

Human impacts causing changes in the carbon cycle – Farming practices and changing land-use

Farming, and resulting changes to the carbon cycle, is a complex tangle of **sinks** and **sources**. In its nature, the growth of vegetation removes CO_2 from the atmosphere through photosynthesis, enabling the **biological sequestration** in plants and soil. In all, this could be a significant carbon sink, however, agricultural practices geared to **mass production**—which is needed to cater for our ever expanding, increasingly wealthy and demanding population—means that agriculture is in fact a source of CO_2.

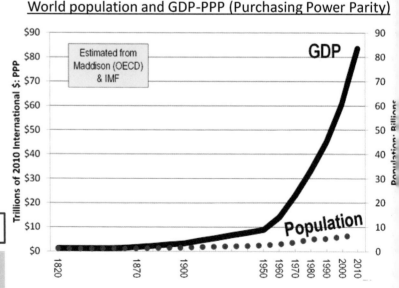

World population and GDP-PPP (Purchasing Power Parity)

Source: W Cox, 2012

YOUR LEARNING TASK:

Using the figure (*right*) outline how population and wealth might impact agriculture and the carbon cycle.

Changing land-use, from natural ecosystems to those designed for human use (including agriculture and pasture), reduce the carbon storage. For example, the **biodiversity** in forest or woodland can sequester significantly more carbon than **monoculture**; crops being the most extreme type of monoculture as any other unwanted plant or animal life is removed.

🔑 **Monoculture** is the cultivation of 1 type of crop on agricultural land

In addition to this it is important to understand that soil is a vast store of carbon. Humus, or organic carbon, gives soil the dark colour and is accumulated over time, through growth and de-composition which adds to the soil. An essential part of **arable farming** is the tilling and ploughing of the land (*shown below*).

This process exposes humus to oxygen and the sunlight causing it to release carbon into the atmosphere. It is claimed that *'on a world-wide basis, from the time agriculture began, almost 80 million tons of carbon have been released from the soil (Rattan Lal, soil scientist, Ohio State University). Up until the late 1950s, ploughing released more carbon dioxide into the atmosphere than all the burning of oil and coal in history.'* (Hofstrand, 2007)

Changing diets, population growth and wealth have led to an increase in meat and dairy consumption, therefore increasing **pastoral farming**. The amount of meat we consume adds significantly to the carbon cycle through a number of ways; Each pound (lb) of beef requires 20lb of grain; Respiration combined with the complex digestive system of cows generates carbon dioxide and methane (which is 1 part carbon to 5 parts hydrogen);

Source: http://www.chinadaily.com.cn/world/2009-06/24/content_8315691.htm

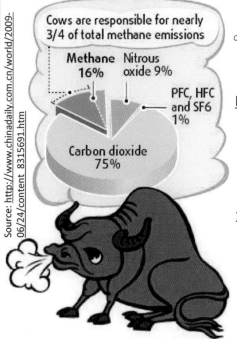

Cows are responsible for nearly 3/4 of total methane emissions

Methane 16% Nitrous oxide 9%

PFC, HFC and SF6 1%

Carbon dioxide 75%

Illustration by Li Zhengming
Source: Reuters   Graphic by Kinyen Pong

Increased demand requires more intensive farming methods, but also more land for both crops and cattle, which has lead to **deforestation**, resulting in a loss of carbon storage capacity and the release of carbon into the atmosphere.

Changes in farming practices and consumer demands has also led to the increased use of fossil fuels within farming. The reasons for this increase is due to the **mechanisation** of agriculture. Wider use of machinery are needed as practices include more complex processes, through the applications of pesticides and fertilisers for example.

Although a less direct link, the transportation, refrigeration and packaging of agricultural products are also contemporary aspects of agricultural practices. This has further increased consumption of fossil fuels and production of carbon into the atmosphere.

= 5523 miles

OpenGameArt.org

Further reading resources:

http://www.chinadaily.com.cn/world/2009-06/24/content_8315691.htm

http://www.agmrc.org/renewable-energy/climate-change/energy-agriculture-carbon-farming/

http://www.treehugger.com/green-food/6-ways-agriculture-impacts-global-warming.html

Be aware, when researching agriculture and its impacts, many further reading resources will make reference to '**carbon dioxide equivalent**'. This does not necessarily relate to the amount of carbon, but is a conversion of other greenhouse gases into a common denominator, so that impacts on global warming can be measured and understood more universally. For example, methane is an especially potent greenhouse gas with up to 25 times more global warming potential than carbon dioxide. So, 1 ton of methane has the same effect on global warming as 25 tons of carbon dioxide. When focussing upon the carbon cycle it is important to remember that carbon dioxide equivalents do not relate to actual quantities of carbon specifically.

Human impacts causing changes in the carbon cycle – Deforestation

Atmospheric CO$_2$

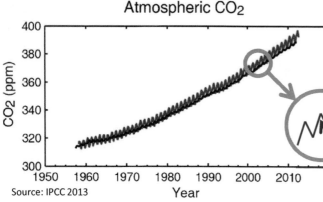

Source: IPCC 2013

As previously mentioned (*page 28*), carbon dioxide in the atmosphere is increasing. With the incorporation of data gathered from atmospheric readings, instead of just ice core data, the amount of CO$_2$ can be tracked more precisely. The result is this 'zig zag' that plots the natural fluxes that occur due to **seasonality**.

In spring time rates of photosynthesis increase as trees leaf out and vegetation springs forth with warming temperatures.

Conversely, in autumn levels of CO$_2$ increase as vegetation becomes less productive and dead leaves fall, plants decay and decompose.

This graphic goes someway in highlighting the importance of woodland and levels of carbon in the atmosphere. What it fails to show is the amount of CO$_2$ absorbed by trees that are not seasonal. For example coniferous forests or tropical rainforest (some of which may have some variation due to wet/dry seasons), which generally bloom through-out the year with no pronounced seasons to impact carbon cycling.

"Deforestation and forest degradation contribute 15 to 20 percent of global carbon emissions, and most of that contribution comes from tropical regions." (NASA, 2011)

As we know, the **biological** component of the carbon cycle, which relates closely to the **nutrient cycle**, is essential in the short-term recycling of carbon between the atmosphere and the lithosphere. Trees, with their supporting **biodiversity**, are an essential part of this process and as a result absorb approximately 120 Gigatons of carbon per year. Some of this carbon is stored (sequestered) and some is released (approximately 60 Gigatons per year) through respiration and decomposition etc. Deforestation is interfering with these natural cycles, ultimately reducing the amount absorbed and releasing carbon stored as biomass and in the soil.

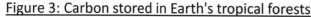

Figure 3: Carbon stored in Earth's tropical forests

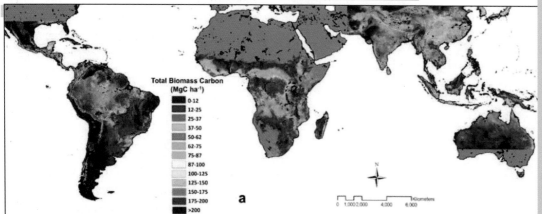

Total Biomass Carbon (MgC ha^{-1})
- 0-12
- 12-25
- 25-37
- 37-50
- 50-62
- 62-75
- 75-87
- 87-100
- 100-125
- 125-150
- 150-175
- 175-200
- >200

a

Rates of respiration and decomposition will also be changed as food webs and nutrient cycles are broken.

Further reading resource:
http://earthobservatory.nasa.gov/Features/CarbonCycle/?src=features-fromthearchives

Figure 4: Annual Deforestation Rates

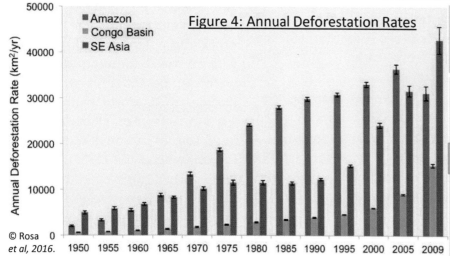

■ Amazon
■ Congo Basin
■ SE Asia

© Rosa et al, 2016.

EXAM PRACTICE:

Using figure 3 and 4, and your own knowledge; assess the impacts of deforestation on the carbon cycle.

[6 marks]

Human impacts causing changes in the carbon cycle – Land use change

Through the study of human impacts on the carbon cycle, it is clear that man is modifying the natural environment at a phenomenal rate. Economic development and population growth are the underlying cause for land-use change, which ultimately can be associated with the growth of agriculture, use of fossil fuels and the causes of deforestation, which have all been outlined on previous pages.

Deforestation and changing land-use: Deforestation is the removal of trees and forest from the land. Many reasons for doing this are to transform the land so that I can be used for another purpose.

- **Subsistence** and **commercial agriculture** combined are the largest cause of deforestation. Land is transformed, in many cases, through the '**slash and burn**' of thousands of acres, turning it into **grassland** for cattle to graze; vast plantations of **cash crops** like soya, palm oil, coffee etc; and into relative small holdings to enable the landless poor to provide for themselves and their families (**subsistence farming**). As discussed on page 29, this reduces storage capacity and releases carbon into the atmosphere.

YOUR LEARNING TASK:

Revise theory linked to agriculture and use of fossil fuels, then outline the ways in which this has changed land-use over time.

(Use 'deforestation and changing land-use' as a guide if you're unsure.)

Figure X: Main causes of rainforest destruction based on multiple information sources*

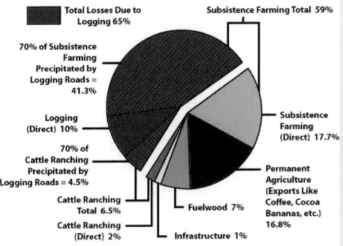

Total Losses Due to Logging 65%

Subsistence Farming Total 59%

70% of Subsistence Farming Precipitated by Logging Roads = 41.3%

Logging (Direct) 10%

70% of Cattle Ranching Precipitated by Logging Roads = 4.5%

Cattle Ranching Total 6.5%

Cattle Ranching (Direct) 2%

Subsistence Farming (Direct) 17.7%

Permanent Agriculture (Exports Like Coffee, Cocoa Bananas, etc.) 16.8%

Fuelwood 7%

Infrastructure 1%

*Based on information from the United Nations Food and Agriculture Organization, World Wildlife Fund, World Resources Institute and Woods Hole Oceanographic Institute.

Source:http://www.rainforestrelief.org/documents/Causes_of_RF_Destruction.gif

Further reading resource:

http://kids.mongabay.com/elementary/505b.html

http://www.rainforestfoundation.org/

http://amazonwatch.org/news/2016/0406-drilling-towards-disaster-ecuadors-aggressive-amazonian-oil-push

- Other land-use changes linked with deforestation are **logging** and the associated **infrastructure** required to facilitate the removal of trees. Once roads and access routes are created, they enable other activities to infiltrate dense tropical rainforests. The most common being settlements with subsistence farming and collection of fuelwood.
- Growth of manufacturing and industry require a vast array of raw materials, many of which lay in the ground. For example, the **Amazon rainforest** is rich in precious metals such as gold, bauxite, copper, tin, manganese, nickel and iron. Mining of these minerals strips back the forest (through **open cast mining** in many cases), contaminating the land, as water and chemicals are used to extract the precious metals. This is exacerbated by clearance for infrastructure like roads and homes for their workforce. Furthermore, vast reserves of oil and gas have also been discovered under these rich carbon sinks. As humans insatiable appetite for fossil fuels continues, and easily accessible reserves deplete, the protection of these areas becomes increasingly difficult; this can be exemplified through the exploitation of oil in the **Yasuni National Park** in Ecuador's Amazon rainforest. Exploitation like this releases carbon in both biological and geological stores.

YOUR LEARNING TASK:

(not covered in directly in this study guide)

As part of the case study development required for 3.1.1.6 on the AQA specification;
Use the further reading links, along with some of your own research to create a **case study** on:
- ❏ Deforestation in the Amazon
- ❏ Oil extraction in the Amazon's Yasuni National Park.
- ❏ Link environmental changes and human activity to <u>impacts</u> upon the **carbon** and **water cycles**.

Urbanisation and the carbon cycle:

The population of the planet has grown exponentially in the last 100 years. To meet the needs of an expanding population, towns and cities have grown. In fact, the urban population has grown from 746 million in 1950, to 3.9 billion in 2014. This is expected to continue rise to 5.4 billion by 2050 (UN 2014).

Tokyo by Sepavo via Flickr

The most obvious links between this urbanisation and the carbon cycle are associated with the creation and consumption of energy and food; the sheer quantities of waste produced, and the amount of land converted into these concrete jungles (huge areas of land that were once carbon sinks but are now sources of carbon). All of these points can be linked to deforestation, agriculture and the burning of fossil fuels within this section, however, it is important to consider that at the heart of all built environments are the materials required to create them.

'**Concrete** is the second most consumed substance on Earth after water, with each person consuming, on average, 3 tons.'

(Rubenstein 2012). **Cement** is the key ingredient in concrete and it is made by heating **limestone** and other materials, like clay, to extreme temperatures (1,400°C) before adding gypsum. The process of heating causes a chemical reaction called '**calcination**' which causes the release of large amounts of CO_2 - approximately 5% of all carbon dioxide emissions can be attributed to the cement industry.

However, it important to note that the '**carbonation**' by concrete structures means that the built environment can also absorb and therefore act as a sink for CO_2. The balance between release and sequestration is contested and, as yet, cannot be labelled **carbon neutral**.

Further reading resource:

https://esa.un.org/unpd/wup/Publications/Files/WUP2014-Highlights.pdf
http://blogs.ei.columbia.edu/2012/05/09/emissions-from-the-cement-industry/
http://www.cement.org/for-concrete-books-learning/concrete-technology/concrete-design-production/concrete-as-a-carbon-sink

Challenge resource: http://journal.frontiersin.org/article/10.3389/fevo.2015.00144/full

YOUR LEARNING TASK:

For **human impacts causing change to the carbon cycle** note down all the keywords in **bold**.
Write a narrative to sum up the human impacts using every key word identified.

EXAM PRACTICE:

Using all the information from pages 27 – 32;

Evaluate which human impact is the most significant cause of change in the carbon cycle.

[20 marks]

Specification links

What is the carbon budget?

'Budgets' and 'budgeting' is probably a phrase you will come to understand well as you get older. In a generic sense we relate it to money and it is used to calculate how much we have to spend based on our income and expenditures.

When relating to the **carbon budget** we are simply replacing the idea of money with carbon! The overall outcome is to limit levels of CO_2 in the atmosphere, so that temperature rise is limited to no more than 2°C above pre-industrial levels (IPCC). The scientific community have quantified this budget as 1 trillion tonnes of carbon (1,000 PgC). In order to stay within the carbon budget we, the global community, now need to reduce the amount of carbon emitted (carbon spending) and increase the amount of carbon stored (carbon savings). Since the Industrial Revolution (1761-1880) the amount of carbon dioxide in the atmosphere has risen to 515 PgC in 2011, this is 52% of the budget already (WRI).

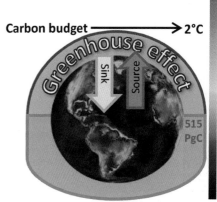

Why do we need a carbon budget? The atmosphere...

The reason we need a carbon budget is because of the **'Enhanced Greenhouse Effect'**.

The **greenhouse effect** is a natural process in which the atmosphere (which naturally contains gases such as carbon dioxide, methane, water vapour, and nitrous oxide), keeps the planet warm. The Greenhouse gases (GHG's) allow the **short-wave radiation** from the Sun to travel directly to the Earth's surface, however, when the heat energy is reradiated from the Earth's surface, as **long-wave radiation**, the greenhouses gases absorb and trap some of this heat energy. This process is extremely important and without it our planet would be approximately 33°C colder (NASA, 1998) and uninhabitable by life as we know it.

As humans have developed, and the population has expanded, we have engaged in a number of activities that are adding more greenhouse gases to the atmosphere, including some synthetic, man-made gases such as CFC's, that work in a similar way to natural GHG's. As concentrations of GHG's (the most notable being carbon dioxide and methane) increase, the greenhouse effect has been **enhanced** and its ability to capture the long-wave heat energy from the Earth's surface has increased. This **anthropogenically** induced warming is the biggest environmental issue facing our planet today. The extent to which the climate changes will dictate the severity of impacts, upon people, and the environment, across the globe.

YOUR LEARNING TASK:

Using the information above, and suggested further reading on the Greenhouse Effect;

Draw an annotated diagram to illustrate how this process works naturally and how it is enhanced anthropogenically.

Further reading resource:

The carbon budget;

http://www.wri.org/ipcc-infographics

The Greenhouse Effect;

https://www.ipcc.ch/publications_and_data/ar4/wg1/en/faq-1-3.html

http://www.bgs.ac.uk/discoveringGeology/climateChange/CCS/greenhouseEffect.html

EXAM PRACTICE:

Explain the links between the **greenhouse effect** and the **carbon cycle**.   [4 marks]

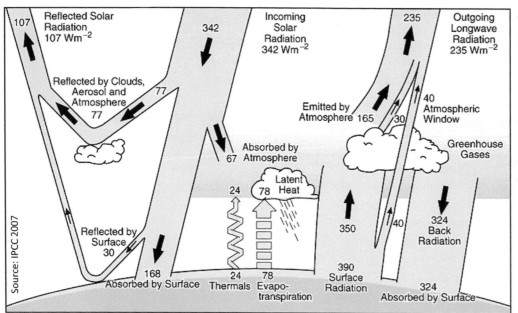

Source: IPCC 2007

This schematic diagram illustrates how the Greenhouse Effect works in relation to the Earth's annual mean energy balance. *'Of the incoming solar radiation, 49% is absorbed by the surface. That heat is returned to the atmosphere as sensible heat, as evapo-transpiration (latent heat) and as thermal infrared radiation. Most of this radiation is absorbed by the atmosphere, which in turn emits radiation both up and down. The radiation lost to space comes from cloud tops and atmospheric regions much colder than the surface.'* (Kiehl et al, 1997)

In order to fully understand and effectively your apply knowledge, for the remainder of the water and carbon cycles topic, it is essential that the concepts surrounding the Greenhouse Effect and its enhancement are fully understood.

As suggested in the previous section, the amount of **carbon** will change the **temperature** of the planet though the **Enhanced Greenhouse Effect**. However, this is just one change that could happen as a result of more carbon moving through the cycle. These next sections explore how increased carbon, and also global temperature, could influence the **land**, **ocean** and **atmosphere**.

Exceeding the carbon budget? Land

The **land** the most important facet of the carbon cycle, because carbon moves between the rocks, soil, permafrost and plants. Therefore when considering increased carbon on the land there are numerous factors which could result in both **positive** and **negative feedback mechanisms** for the carbon cycle and global climate.

As the amount of carbon in the atmosphere increases, the rates of **photosynthesis** could also increase. In fact *'models predict that plants might grow anywhere from 12 to 76 percent more if atmospheric carbon dioxide is doubled'* (Riebeek, 2011). The increased growth of plants is called **carbon fertilisation** and has the potential to provide a significant **sink** in the carbon cycle.

As shown (*right*) the planet is getting 'greener' as a result of increased levels of carbon dioxide. This demonstrates that higher levels of photosynthesis could provide an important **negative feedback mechanism** to counteract the increasing levels of carbon in the atmosphere.

However, it is important to note that, carbon dioxide is just one component vegetation needs to grow successfully. Therefore, if there is a shortage in water, sunlight or nutrients (like nitrogen) then the increase in photosynthesis will not take place. When considered in context to changing climates, this could nullify this as a negative feedback mechanism.

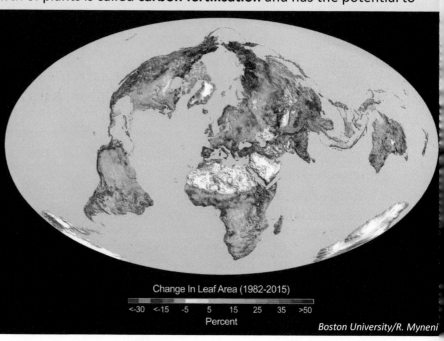

Change In Leaf Area (1982-2015)

<-30 <-15 -5 5 15 25 35 >50
Percent

Boston University/R. Myneni

This image shows the change in leaf area across the globe from 1982-2015

Source: http://www.nasa.gov/feature/goddard/2016/carbon-dioxide-fertilization-greening-earth

Exceeding the carbon budget? Land continued…

There are pools (stores) of carbon on **land,** which are especially sensitive to temperature change. As more heat is trapped in the atmosphere and global temperatures increase, these stores will be released and result in **positive feedback.** The most significant exemplification of this is **permafrost**. Permafrost covers 22% of the land surface, and is defined as the subsurface layer of soil that remains frozen (below 0°C) for 2 consecutive years. It is estimated that approximately 1,672 billion metric tonnes (Schuur et al, 2008) of carbon is stored in the permafrost, which is rich in organic carbon. When temperatures rise, the permafrost thaws allowing the decomposition of the organic matter by microbial activity to increase. As discussed on page 24, this process leads to respiration and the release of carbon dioxide (and some methane) into the atmosphere. It is predicted that *'if just 10 percent of this permafrost were to thaw, it could release enough extra carbon dioxide to the atmosphere to raise temperatures an additional 0.7°C by 2100'* (Riebeek, 2011).

Distribution of permafrost in the Arctic region

Permafrost
- Isolated
- Sporadic
- Discontinuous
- Continuous

Source: https://nsidc.org/cryosphere/frozenground/whereis_fg.html

Source: International Permafrost Association, 1998. Circumpolar Active-Layer Permafrost System (CAPS), version 1.0.

Kari Greer, National Interagency Fire Center

Another **positive feedback** associated with increased global temperatures on **land** is the incidence of **forest and wild fires**. As explored on page 27, forest fires, and wild fires (which includes fire in other vegetated areas, such as brush), could occur more readily as dry conditions make more areas susceptible. The burning process removes sinks and releases stores; and if conditions are so dry, it would hinder the arrival of new vegetation, therefore causing an imbalance in the carbon cycle that adds more CO_2 to the atmosphere, further enhancing the greenhouse effect.

Further reading resources:

Photosynthesis and carbon dioxide:
http://www.nasa.gov/feature/goddard/2016/carbon-dioxide-fertilization-greening-earth

Permafrost:
https://www.theguardian.com/environment/2012/mar/05/permafrost-climate-carbon-emissions

YOUR LEARNING TASK:

Create a mind map to illustrate how changes to the carbon cycle could have impacts on land.

EXAM PRACTICE:

Explain how changes to the carbon cycle on land could lead to positive and negative feedback.

Exceeding the carbon budget? Oceans

As identified on page 25, **oceans** cover the majority of our planet, and are a significant **carbon sink**. It is estimated that they contain 38,000 to 40,000 billion tonnes of carbon, which is the second largest store of carbon on the planet. Furthermore, it is believed that the oceans have absorbed 38% of anthropogenically produced CO_2 (Caldeira et al, 2005). This absorption of carbon dioxide from the atmosphere provides an important buffer that regulates carbon concentrations on the land and in the air. If the amount of carbon in the ocean continues to rise, it could lead to a range of environmental, social and economic repercussions.

YOUR LEARNING TASK:

For each of the impacts on the ocean, outline possible knock-on effects.

Try to add ideas that can be categorised into environmental, social, economic and political effects.

As for all living things, carbon in the oceans is essential. However, the balance and type of carbon is vitally important. As we know, carbon is present in many forms; for example, **calcium carbonate** is used for building shells, corals and bone structures. But **carbonic acid**, which is produced when atmospheric carbon dioxide is dissolved in the ocean; this makes the oceans more **acidic**, and can result in weak and pitted shells. In addition to this, the carbonic acid also reacts with the carbonate ions in the water to create **bicarbonate**. As acidity increases more of the shell building carbonate becomes bicarbonate. This means that shell building creatures, including coral

OCEAN ACIDIFICATION

Source: http://www.oceanacidification.org.uk/

reefs, have to expend more energy resulting in weaker, thinner and more fragile structures. The implications of this on **food webs** could be significant.

So, carbon dioxide in the atmosphere is being absorbed by the oceans, and in doing so it is changing the acidity of the water. To provide some context it is important to note that, even though the oceans have absorbed 500 Gigatons (38%) of anthropogenically produced carbon, ocean pH levels have only decreased by 0.1 at the ocean surface, with no change recorded in deep ocean waters. Despite this seemingly insignificant figure, this pH change represents a 30% increase in acidity in the last 200 years, which is faster than any know change in ocean chemistry in the last 50 million years (NOAA/PMEL).

Increases in CO_2 in the oceans could mean that **phytoplankton** and ocean plants (like sea grasses), which take carbon dioxide directly from the water could benefit.

Much like vegetation on land, these species could become more abundant and in turn have a positive impact on the food chain.

This is especially important because phytoplankton is a **keystone species**, supporting a wide range of life from tiny invertebrates up to multi-ton whales.

The amount of phytoplankton could also provide an important **negative feedback mechanism**, with a greater abundance removing carbon dioxide from the water and moving it through the **biological** and eventually **geological** aspects of the **carbon cycle**.

EXAM PRACTICE:

Explain how ocean acidification is linked to the carbon cycle.

[6 marks]

Further reading resource:

Ocean acidification: http://ocean.si.edu/ocean-acidification

Phytoplankton: http://earthobservatory.nasa.gov/Features/Phytoplankton/page2.php

Food webs: http://sciencelearn.org.nz/Contexts/Life-in-the-Sea/Science-Ideas-and-Concepts/Marine-food-webs

As the global climate increases, so too does the average **temperature** of the oceans. The consequences of this are far reaching and varied. Although useful to explore a range of these consequences, it is important to focus upon changes to carbon dioxide and the carbon cycle as a whole.

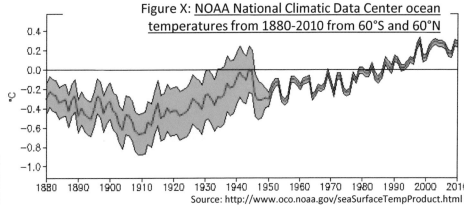

Figure X: <u>NOAA National Climatic Data Center ocean temperatures from 1880-2010 from 60°S and 60°N</u>

Source: http://www.oco.noaa.gov/seaSurfaceTempProduct.html

As discussed on the previous page, although increases in the amount of CO_2 *could* lead to greater abundance of **phytoplankton**, warming oceans could effectively counter this. Phytoplankton, along with zooplankton, are sensitive to water **temperature** and **salinity**; if water temperatures rise and salinity decreases, the amount of these **keystone species** will also diminish. This could create significant **positive feedbacks** as less CO_2 is absorbed and a vital food source is reduced.

The ocean as a carbon sink involves a complex combination of factors that influence how much carbon is absorbed (or released). As a result, it is often unclear what the final results of changes in ocean temperatures will actually mean. For example, warmer oceans have a lower capacity, than cold water, to hold dissolved gases like carbon dioxide. On the other hand, however, increase in the **acidity** of the oceans, caused by CO_2 dissolved in the water, causes a chemical reaction that would mean the oceans can absorb more carbon dioxide. Scientists are researching these complex interactions, but so far the outcomes are far from clear, especially when possible changes to ocean current (*see below*) are also considered.

Warming oceans will, inevitably, lead to the **melting** of ice at the poles. The consequences of this will be significant and varied, but in relation to **global climate**, the most pertinent and important consequence could be 'global cooling'. The theory behind this is linked to **ocean currents**. These transfer heat from the warm equatorial regions, and cold water from the polar regions in a global circulation system, also known as **thermohaline circulation**. The **temperature**, **salinity** and **density** of the water are important factors that drive the 'ocean conveyor belt'. In Europe the **Gulf Stream** is an extremely important ocean current, that dictates the **climate** and

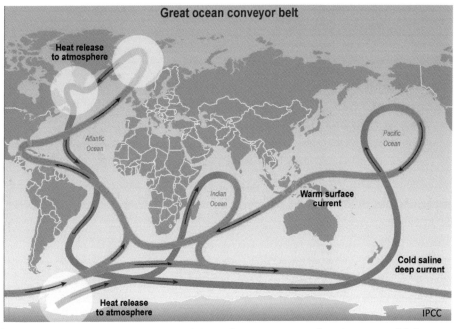

Great ocean conveyor belt

Heat release to atmosphere

Atlantic Ocean

Pacific Ocean

Indian Ocean

Warm surface current

Cold saline deep current

Heat release to atmosphere

IPCC

weather experienced. The fast moving Gulf Stream transports vast quantities of warm water (and warm air) from the Tropics; without it Europe would be between 5 - 10°C colder. The whole system circulates because, as the warm water reaches the Arctic regions, it cools and becomes denser, causing it to sink and travel south towards the Equator. However, if Arctic polar ice melts, it will add large quantities of fresh water. Adding fresh water lowers the salinity and density of the water, which would prevent the 'sink and pull' process that happens in the cold northern reaches of the Gulf Stream. This would effectively 'switch off' the engine for this ocean current. Scientists believe that disruption to global ocean circulation systems would lead to severe temperature decreases in Europe, resulting in the onset of a new ice age. As for the rest of the world, disruption of global ocean currents would affect not only affect the ocean, but also the movement of air masses, which could have riotous and unpredictable outcomes.

specification links

3.1.1.4 Water, carbon, climate and life on Earth
The key role of the carbon and water stores and cycles in supporting life on Earth with particular reference to climate. The relationship between the water cycle and carbon cycle in the atmosphere. The role of feedbacks within and between cycles and their link to climate change and implications for life on Earth.

How do carbon and water cycles support life on Earth? In the beginning...

We have to go back 4.5 billion years to understand how the carbon and water cycle formed the planet we inhabit today. In Earth's formative years it was a mass of molten volatility; volcanoes constantly erupted, releasing carbon dioxide, ammonia and water vapour, as steam, to form a basic atmosphere. At this point there was no life on Earth and no oxygen. However, there was water. Once the water vapour was released from the volcanoes, it rose into the air, where it cooled, condensed and then proceeded to rain. This was no light drizzle, but tremendous rain storms that lasted for thousands of years. All this rainfall, combined with additional water deposited by comets, which bombarded our planet in it's formative years, formed rivers and oceans, and so the water cycle began.

The formation of the oceans was also pivotal to the carbon cycle. Within the oceans simple bacteria developed. Using energy from the sun, and carbon dioxide from the atmosphere, they grew, producing oxygen as a by-product. The addition of oxygen to the atmosphere allowed new species to develop. As these flowed through the carbon cycle, vast quantities of carbon dioxide was sequestered into the land and ocean, creating a balance of gases, in the atmosphere, that is essential to life. It does this through the regulation of the climate and air we need to breathe.

YOUR LEARNING TASK:

Convert this text, about the start of the carbon and water cycles, into a cartoon strip.

Further reading resources:

http://www.bbc.co.uk/science/earth/earth
timeline/earth_formed#p00fzss4

How do carbon and water cycles interact in the atmosphere to influence climate?

The **atmosphere** is the key to the **climate** of the planet. The interactions of both the carbon and water cycle can have a significant influence upon this sphere, and therefore the climate too.

Scientists have been able to identify which wavelengths of energy each greenhouse gas absorbs, along with concentrations in the atmosphere. When these two factors are taken into account, they are able to calculate the influence each gas has on the warming of the planet. These studies have revealed that *'carbon dioxide causes approximately 20 percent of the Earth's greenhouse effect; water accounts for 50 percent and clouds 25 percent'* (Riebeek, 2011).

CO_2 is much more stable compared to water, which changes state within a relatively small temperature range. This means that although there is significantly less CO_2, compared to water vapour and cloud, the changes in CO_2 concentrations are the linchpin that dictates how much

Carbon Dioxide Concentration (Parts Per Million)

pre-industrial carbon dioxide concentration ~280 parts per million

Global Temperature Anomaly (°C)

5-year average

annual average

water vapour and cloud is held in the atmosphere. For example, an increase in CO_2 would cause a rise in temperatures and increase in evaporation. More water vapour is held in the atmosphere, and being a greenhouse gas, enhances the warming further. Alternatively, lower CO_2 would cause cooling, leading to more condensation and precipitation. The water vapour leaves the atmosphere reducing the amount of this greenhouse gas, which in turn leading to further cooling. This interaction leads to **positive feedbacks**, which enhance change.

How do carbon and water cycles interact in the atmosphere to influence climate? Continued…

Based on understanding, developed on previous pages, it should be clear that anthropologic disruption to the carbon cycle is increasing the concentrations of CO_2 in the atmosphere, enhancing the Greenhouse Effect. The trapping of long-wave radiation is raising global temperatures, causing a positive feedback, as more evaporation increases water vapour in the atmosphere. However, this one outcome will have a **multiplier effect** for both the environment and people. These knock on effects are varied and complex, casting a complicated web of **positive** and **negative feedbacks** that make the future difficult to forecast. Despite this, some ideas are outlined below;

- Rising temperatures lead to higher rates of evaporation and evapotranspiration. The warmer air can hold more moisture which will in turn, create clouds and more intense precipitation. For some time, it was believed that more cloud cover could increase the **reflectivity (albedo)** of the planet, leading to a negative feedback that would help counter the enhancement of the greenhouse effect. However, scientists have largely dismissed this idea for two reasons; 1) The intensification of the water cycle could mean that clouds are dissipating quicker; 2) Clouds are containing less ice crystals, which make them significantly less reflective. As a result, a previously believed negative feedback has been turned on its head, causing concern that climate change could spiral at a rate more rapid than previously believed.

- Levels of precipitation, as rainfall, would reduce the amount of snow cover. When combined with overall warming, **albedo** would decrease, while the absorption of the suns energy into the darker surfaces would increase.

- Changes in evaporation and precipitation would directly impact upon the water cycle, and the drainage basin sub-systems within it. Drainage basins could, dependant upon their location, experience;

> An increased in input, due to higher levels of precipitation, which would in turn influence the flows, transfers and discharge. It could be argued that the intensification of precipitation could cause more **rapid run-off**, less storage and movement of water as throughflow and groundwater flow, making some areas more susceptible to **flooding** and **drought**. Conversely, some areas could become more lush and verdant as a result of these changes, reducing seasonal extremes in the **water balance**.

> An increased output, due to higher levels of evaporation and evapotranspiration. These areas would experience a **moisture deficit** that would not only influence the movement of water, but also impact upon the carbon cycle through changes to vegetation growth (*see below*).

- Increased moisture, as the water cycle intensifies, would encourage the growth of vegetation in some areas, and therefore increasing levels of photosynthesis. This would help to regulate levels of carbon dioxide in the atmosphere, which is a negative feedback mechanism. However, an increase in drought conditions in other regions could lead to a decrease in vegetation, which in turn would expose more soil, releasing stored carbon from within it. The area forecast to experience increased

YOUR LEARNING TASK:

Organise these ideas into positive and negative feedback mechanisms.

Further reading resources:

http://earthobservatory.nasa.gov/Features/Water/page3.php

https://www.theguardian.com/environment/2016/apr/07/clouds-climate-change-analysis-liquid-ice-global-warming

http://content.time.com/time/health/article/0,8599,1912448,00.html

EXAM PRACTICE:

Evaluate the impacts, of water and carbon in the atmosphere, upon the climate.
[20 marks]

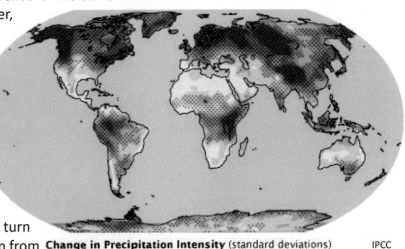

Change in Precipitation Intensity (standard deviations)   IPCC

-1.5   -1   -.5   0   .5   1   1.5

precipitation is greater than that in deficit, however, consideration does need to be paid to land-use, human interaction and other factors associated with climate change that could complicate this initially simple concept.

specification links

In as short a time as a decade, it has become clear that enhancement of the greenhouse effect, and the resultant changes to the climate, are irrefutable. Evidence from a vast array of sources, supported by analysis and evaluation from scientists and scholars around the world, have ensured that this **chronic**, **context hazard** is gaining the attention it deserves. Without any ambiguity, it is clear that the amount of carbon dioxide we are adding to the atmosphere is **unsustainable**. If we want our children, and our children's children, to experience the planet and enjoy a good quality of life, then we need to take action to **adapt** and **mitigate** the impacts of climate change.

Greenhouse gases have lifespans, in the atmosphere, that mean gases added during the **Industrial Revolution** could still be influencing the climate today.

Carbon dioxide can remain in the atmosphere for as little as 5 years, but on average has a lifespan of 100-300 years (Blasing, 2016). This is the longest lifespan of all the greenhouse gases.

We cannot undo the last two centuries of carbon dioxide emission, however, we can reduce the amount of carbon dioxide we release and increase storage. The aim is to limited climate change to a rise of 2°C, in the hope that we can prevent the most extreme consequences.

What is mitigation?

Common terms associated with dealing with climate change are **adaptation** and **mitigation**. **Adaptation** refers to the ways in which we can cope with the changes that occur as a result of climate change, in order to lower our vulnerability. For example, building flood defences or developing drought resistant crops. However, none of the strategies of adaptation deal with the source of the problem, this is where mitigation comes in. Rather than just reacting, **mitigation** is about pro-actively reducing the cause of the problem in order to try to minimise the effects.

Further reading resource: https://www.theguardian.com/environment/2012/jan/16/greenhouse-gases-remain-air

How can we fix climate change? Mitigation strategies...

For this course, you need to be able to identify and describe a range of human interventions to reduce or prevent carbon emissions, that can be categorised into local, regional, national, global strategies. Some examples of each have been provided in this study guide, however, use the further reading and learning task to develop your independent study skills to further your own understanding.

Global action on climate change first came about in 1992, with the creation of the United Nations Framework Convention on Climate Change (**UNFCCC**). This international treaty now has 195 members, who focus upon adaption, mitigation, finance and technology. The **Kyoto Protocol** (1997) was an extension of this treaty to set agreements on quantified reductions of emissions within specific timeframes. The most recent round of agreements and commitments centred around the **Paris Agreements** (COP21). The **IPCC** (Intergovernmental Panel on Climate Change) is an international group, established by branches of the UN (UNEP, WMO), to provide a clear scientific view on climate change and the possible consequences it may have. The work of the IPCC is used to facilitate meaningful international action by UNFCCC members at global, national, regional and local levels.

YOUR LEARNING TASK:

Using the further reading suggested below, make notes on the outcomes of COP21, and the international agreements linked to dealing with climate change.

Further reading resources:

http://www.bbc.co.uk/news/science-environment-24021772
http://newsroom.unfccc.int/
https://www.ipcc.ch/news_and_events/docs/factsheets/FS_what_ipcc.pdf
http://www.unep.org/climatechange/

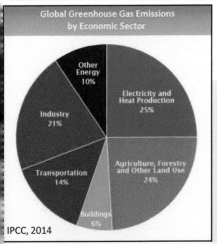

Global Greenhouse Gas Emissions by Economic Sector

Other Energy 10%
Electricity and Heat Production 25%
Industry 21%
Agriculture, Forestry and Other Land Use 24%
Transportation 14%
Buildings 6%

IPCC, 2014

Energy production is a major contributor to the enhanced greenhouse effect, in fact, 41% of all carbon dioxide emissions are released from the energy sector (World Bank, 2014). Therefore, it stands to reason, that reducing emissions from this sector is vital to effectively mitigate the effects of climate change.

An obvious strategy, to minimise CO_2 emissions, is to make away from power stations which burn **fossil fuels**, like coal and gas. The use of **renewable** sources of energy has grown, to approximately 19% of global energy consumption in 2015 (REN21, 2016). Renewable energy sources have vast potential and, as yet, are still under-utilised.

Warwick Sweeney

Carbon Capture and Sequestration (CCS)

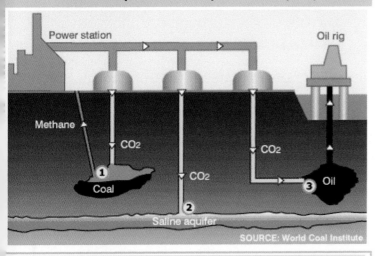

Power station
Oil rig
Methane
CO_2
① Coal
CO_2
CO_2
②
③ Oil
Saline aquifer

SOURCE: World Coal Institute

The concept behind **carbon capture and storage** (sequestration) is simple; collect the carbon emissions from the source, transport, and store it underground. In all, CCS could capture over 90% of carbon dioxide emissions from power plants, heavy industry and refineries. Overall it has the potential to reduce 50% of global CO_2 emissions, with estimated underground storage capacity of 2000 trillion tonnes (IPCC).

However, as it can be, with things that sound simple, there are lots of complex processes involved, leading to concerns about its viability and success. The key issues surrounding the capturing and compression of CO_2 are; the additional energy required for the process; the significant financial cost, which would raise the price of energy for consumers; and concerns linked to CO_2 leakage from the sequestration process.

Further reading resources:

http://www.ccsassociation.org/what-is-ccs/

https://www.theguardian.com/environment/carbon-capture-and-storage

http://hub.globalccsinstitute.com/sites/default/files/publications/191088/fact%20sheet%20what%20is%20ccs.pdf

Changing rural land-use - Agriculture

Meeting the needs of a rapidly expanding population means putting food on the table. As a result, 11% of the globe's land surface is used in crop production (FAO).

When crops are cultivated and soil is exposed (for example, once a crop is harvested), oxidisation and radiation from the Sun, release carbon from the soil into the atmosphere. When combined with intensive farming methods, that favour **monoculture** and strict control over what grows/lives in the fields, **agricultural land** has become a source, rather than a sink of CO_2.

However, research into farming practices has revealed that, relatively simple changes in agricultural practices could have big impacts in terms of carbon sequestration. Organic farming is a practice that refrains from using pesticides, herbicides and industrial fertilisers, combined with crop rotation and systems that integrate livestock, promote biodiversity in soil. In addition to this, it also provides year wide crop cover that shields the soil, increases rates of sequestration into the soil through the roots of plants and minimises interruption of CO_2 recycling through photosynthesis.

These changes to agricultural practice do not require complex technologies, but simply a return to more traditional farming methods. In addition to reducing carbon in the atmosphere, it would improve soil quality, protecting land from degradation and **desertification**, which is a growing global concern. However, it does contradict modern farming practices where productivity and profit margins are driving forces.

YOUR LEARNING TASK:

Draw a flow diagram of carbon cycling, that compares intensive, monoculture farming to more traditional organic farming practices.

How can we fix climate change? Mitigation strategies continued…

Changing rural land-use - Afforestation

Further reading:

Deforestation, and resultant changes to land-use (*see pages 30 – 31*), are having a significant impact on carbon dioxide levels in the atmosphere. Changes in land-use from previous forested areas, are releasing carbon and lowering rates of photosynthesis. Scientists estimate that, forest ecosystems store up to 100 times more carbon than agricultural fields of the same area. Overall, it is estimated that more than 1.5 Gigatons (Gt) of carbon dioxide is released into the atmosphere due to deforestation, mainly the cutting and burning of forests, every year.

To reverse some of the negative impacts of deforestation, planting new forests and protecting current forested areas seems like a most obvious answer. In relation to carbon, rates of afforestation and reforestation has sequestered 1.1-1.6 Gt per year, which is about 2 percent of the annual global carbon uptake by the terrestrial biosphere (IPCC, 2000).

With more management, that prevents overall loss of forested areas; carbon storage could be increased, carbon cycling from the atmosphere would increase and wood could be used as a carbon neutral source of energy that could alleviate the reliance on problematic, carbon rich, fossil fuels.

YOUR LEARNING TASK:

Using the further reading suggestions and your own research, make notes on global and national strategies linked to afforestation and forest conservation.

Agriculture:

http://e360.yale.edu/feature/soil_as_carbon_storehouse_new_weapon_in_climate_fight/2744/

http://www.ucsusa.org/sites/default/files/legacy/assets/documents/food_and_agriculture/ag-carbon-sequest-fact-sheet.pdf

Afforestation: http://www.un-redd.org/

http://www.worldwildlife.org/threats/deforestation

Improved transport practices

20 percent of all CO_2 emissions, generated from the combustion of fossil fuels, is caused by transportation (World Bank, 2014).

When combined with a growing global population and increase in wealth, especially in industrialising countries, car ownership is expected to continue to rise.

Andrei Makhonin

As a result, reducing emissions and encouraging alternative sources of transportation will play a key role in mitigating climate change.

In general, new technologies, such as low emission vehicles, hybrids (which combine internal combustion engines with electric motors), and vehicles with hydrogen fuel cells are becoming much more widespread. The development of these vehicles are encouraged by government policies, designed to meet agreements under UNFCCC (like the Kyoto Protocol, and more recently COP21) and also increasing consumer demand, as people are becoming more conscious of environmental issues and their predicted consequences.

Another large part of this mitigation strategy is to encourage the use of public transport and non-motorised transport, like cycling and walking. These are facilitated through national and regional schemes such as policies, like taxation on cars, subsidies/grants and infrastructure planning; for example the introduction of cycle lanes.

YOUR LEARNING TASK:

Using the links below, and your own research, create a case study on improved transport in Curitiba.

https://www.theguardian.com/cities/2015/may/26/curitiba-brazil-brt-transport-revolution-history-cities-50-buildings

http://www.coolgeography.co.uk/A-level/AQA/Year%2013/World%20Cities/Sustainability/Curitiba.htm

Further reading resources:

http://www.alternative-energy-news.info/technology/transportation/

https://www.cyclescheme.co.uk/

And finally...

Please find some **additional reading links** for the carbon cycle. These suggested readings draw together learning through-out the carbon cycle topic, to explore and develop key processes, interactions, consequences and strategies.

http://www.climatechange2013.org/images/report/WG1AR5_Chapter08_FINAL.pdf

https://www.ipcc.ch/publications_and_data/ar4/syr/en/spms4.html

http://www.unep.org/climatechange/mitigation/Home/tabid/104335/Default.aspx

EXAM PRACTICE AND APPLICATION OF UNDERSTANDING:

Explain the terms sink, store and source in relation to the carbon cycle.   [6 marks]

Explain why the volumes of carbon transferred varies at sere level.   [4 marks]

Using the carbon cycle systems diagram (*page 24*), explain how the nutrient and rock cycle sub-systems differ?

Explain how the carbon cycle can vary as a result of natural processes.   [6 marks]

Using pages 27 – 32;
Evaluate and explain which human impact is having the greatest impact on the carbon cycle.   [20 marks]

Using your own case study example (see page X), explain how one human activity is impacting both the carbon and water cycle.

What is the carbon budget, and why is it important?

Explain how the greenhouse effect is being enhanced by human activity.

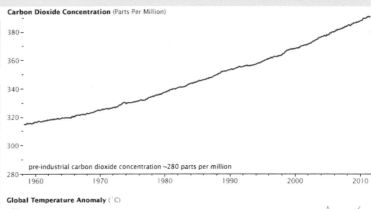

Using the graphs (right), explain how water and carbon cycles interact to influence the climate.

Outline the ways in which changes to the carbon cycle will lead to positive feedbacks for the global climate.

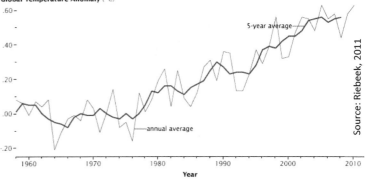

How are people mitigating climate change at a national level?

Explain why global mitigation strategies are vital.

Assess the importance of the ocean relation to the water and carbon cycles.   [20 marks]

What is Still left to do?

These are the elements of the 'water and carbon cycle' topic that are <u>not</u> covered in this study guide, however, **you will need to know these for the exam**.

specification links

3.1.1.5 Quantitative and qualitative skills
Students must engage with a range of quantitative and relevant qualitative skills, within the theme water and carbon cycles. Students must specifically understand simple mass balance, unit conversions and the analysis and presentation of field data.

3.1.1.6 Case studies
Case study of a tropical rainforest setting to illustrate and analyse key themes in water and carbon cycles and their relationship to environmental change and human activity.

See pages 31 and 43 for the learning task and knowledge check linked to this requirement of the specification.

3.1.1.6 Case studies
Case study of a river catchment(s) at a local scale to illustrate and analyse the key themes studies so far, engage with field data and consider the impact of precipitation upon drainage basin stores and transfers and implications for sustainable water supply and/or flooding.

Glossary

Some key terms have been added, to aid your study. However, many key terms are still missing their meanings in relation to the water and carbon cycle. As part of your on-going revision complete the glossary using meanings embedded in the text and your own research.

Term	Definition
Abstraction	
Adapt	To make changes in order to cope with, or become less vulnerable to, a problem or issue.
Albedo	
Anthropogenically	Caused by human activity.
Arable farming	
Atmosphere	
Aquifer	This is a store of water in permeable rocks underground. Aquifers can be 'confined' or 'unconfined'. Water is extracted from aquifers using wells.
Biodiversity	
Biological	
Biosphere	
Calcination	
Carbonation	This is the chemical reaction that causes the absorption of carbon dioxide into concrete.
Carbon budget	
Carbon fertilisation	
Carbon neutral	
Carbon sink	
Cash crops	This is a crop that is grown due to it's commercial value. For example, cotton, tobacco and cocoa.
Catchment area	
Cement	This is the key ingredient in concrete. It is manufactured by heating limestone & other materials, like clay, to extremely high temperatures. This process causes **calcination**.
Chronic hazard	These are events or hazards that have the ability to cause further widespread and/or long term risks and problems, for example through positive feedback mechanisms.
Climate	

Glossary

Some key terms have been added, to aid your study. However, many key terms are still missing their meanings in relation to the water and carbon cycle. As part of your on-going revision complete the glossary using meanings embedded in the text and your own research.

Closed system	
Condensation	
Coniferous	These are the mostly evergreen trees and shrubs that usually have needle-shaped leaves. Examples of coniferous trees are pines, firs and spruces.
Context hazard	These are hazards that have widespread threats, with the potential to affect the entire planet.
Cryosphere	
Deciduous	
Decomposition	
Desertification	This is the process by which once fertile land becomes desert. See http://www.greenfacts.org/en/desertification/ for more information.
Dew Point	This is the atmospheric temperature (which varies according to pressure and humidity) below which water droplets begin to condense and dew can form.
Discharge	
Drought	
Dynamic equilibrium	
Enhanced greenhouse effect	
Evaporation	
Evapotranspiration	
Feedback	
Flood	
Flood hydrograph	
Food webs	
Fossil fuel	

Glossary

Some key terms have been added, to aid your study. However, many key terms are still missing their meanings in relation to the water and carbon cycle. As part of your on-going revision complete the glossary using meanings embedded in the text and your own research.

Term	Meaning
Geological	This refers to the non-living or inorganic component of the carbon cycle. This is linked to the formation and sequestration of carbon in rocks, which can take millions of years.
Greenhouse effect	
Greenhouse gases	
Groundwater	This is water that occurs below the surface of the ground, where all the pore spaces in the subsurface material are completely filled with water.
Hazard	This is an event which has the potential to threaten both life and property.
Hydrocarbons	
Hydrosphere	
Impermeable	
Industrialisation	
Industrial Revolution	A time of rapid change, where mechanisation of labour led to dramatic increase in productivity. This term is often refers to changes in England (from the late 1700's onwards), where steam power led to dramatic shifts in industry.
Infiltration	
Infrastructure	
Inorganic	This refers to the 'non-living' components of the carbon cycle.
Inputs	
Interception	
IPCC	
Irrigation	
Keystone species	
Latent heat	
Leaching	This refers to the washing out and removal of minerals from the soil.

Glossary

Some key terms have been added, to aid your study. However, many key terms are still missing their meanings in relation to the water and carbon cycle. As part of your on-going revision complete the glossary using meanings embedded in the text and your own research.

Lithosphere	
Mechanisation	
Mitigation	Pro-actively reducing the cause of the problem in order to try to minimise the effects.
Monoculture	This refers to the cultivation of a single crop on a farm or region.
Multiplier effect	
Negative feedback	
Non-renewable resource	
Nutrient cycle	
Open cast mining	
Open system	
Organic	
Outputs	
Pastoral farming	
Percolation	This is the downward movement of water through the soil to get deeper underground.
Permafrost	
Pervious	An example of a pervious rock is limestone. It allows the water to move through the cracks and faults in the rock.
Photosynthesis	
Phytoplankton	
Positive feedback	
Precipitation	
Processes	These are actions and movements within the system. It is a general term that can also include **flows** and **transfers**.

Glossary

Some key terms have been added, to aid your study. However, many key terms are still missing their meanings in relation to the water and carbon cycle. As part of your on-going revision complete the glossary using meanings embedded in the text and your own research.

Term	Meaning
Relief	In geography, this refers to the shape of the land, for example, the highest and lowest elevations.
Renewable resource	
Respiration	
River regime	This is the variability of a river's discharge, throughout the course of a year, due to precipitation, temperature, evapotranspiration, and the characteristics of the drainage basin.
Rock cycle	
Salinity	This refers to salt content, for example in water or soil.
Saturated	
Seasonality	
Sedimentary rock	
Sequestration	This is the removal and storage of carbon dioxide from the atmosphere. This can occur naturally: photosynthesis – respiration = sequestration or can be linked to human intervention where CO_2 is captured and then stored (CCS).
Sere	This refers to a community of plants at any given stage of succession. For example, you may compare equatorial rainforest to tundra to reveal differences in volumes of carbon transfer.
Short-wave radiation	
Soil moisture budget	
Slash and burn	
Stemflow	
Stock resource	This refers to a resource for which there is a fixed quantity available.
Subsistence farming	
Sub-system	This is a system that can be found within another. For example, within the water cycle, a global system, there are drainage basins. These are much smaller, localised systems of water inputs, flows/transfers and outputs.
Surface water	

Glossary

Some key terms have been added, to aid your study. However, many key terms are still missing their meanings in relation to the water and carbon cycle. As part of your on-going revision complete the glossary using meanings embedded in the text and your own research.

Sustainable	Meeting the needs of the present, without compromising the ability of future generations, to meet their own needs. To do something in a way that will last and not destroy it for the future.
System	This is a process or collection of **processes** that transforms **inputs** into **outputs**.
Thermal expansion	
Thermohaline circulation	
Throughflow	
Tributary	
Unsustainable	
Uplift	In geology this refers to the vertical elevation of the Earth's surface, in response to natural causes, such as movement of plate tectonics.
Urbanisation	
Water balance	
Water deficit	
Watershed	
Weather	
Weathering	

References + Acknowledgements

The author would like to thank the following for their permission to use photographs or other copyright materials. Every effort has been made to contact copyright holders of material reproduced in this book. Any omissions will be rectified in subsequent printings if notice is given to the author.

BBC Bitesize http://www.bbc.co.uk/bitesize/standard/physics/energy_matters/heat_in_the_home/revision/3 [Accessed: 07/2016]. T. Blasing, April 2016. 'Carbon Dioxide Information Analysis Centre: Recent Greenhouse Gas Concentrations.' http://cdiac.esd.ornl.gov/pns/current_ghg.html [Accessed: 08/2016]. T. Boden, G. Marland, and R.J. Andres, 2010. 'Global, Regional, and National Fossil-Fuel CO_2 Emissions.' Carbon Dioxide Information Analysis Center, Oak Ridge National Laboratory, U.S. Department of Energy, Oak Ridge, Tenn., U.S.A. doi 10.3334/CDIAC/00001_V2010.[Accessed: 08/2016]. Boston University/R. Myneni http://www.nasa.gov/feature/goddard/2016/carbon-dioxide-fertilization-greening-earth [Accesses: 08/2016]. BP data. 'Primary energy - 2015 in review'© 1996-2016 BP p.l.c http://www.bp.com/en/global/corporate/energy-economics/statistical-review-of-world-energy/primary-energy.html [Accessed: 07/2016]. K. Caldeira, M. Akai, P. Brewer, B.Chen, P. Haugan, T. Iwama, P. Johnston, H. Kheshgi, Q. Li, T. Ohsumi, H. Pörtner, C. Sabine, Y. Shirayama, J. Thomson, 2005. 'Ocean Storage. IPCC Special Report on Carbon dioxide Capture and Storage.' https://www.ipcc.ch/pdf/special-reports/srccs/srccs_chapter6.pdf [Accessed: 08/2016]. © Greg Carley, 2009. W Cox, 2012. 'The expanding economic pie and grinding poverty.' http://www.newgeography.com/content/003271-the-expanding-economic-pie-grinding-poverty [Accessed: 08/2016] http://dilu.bol.ucla.edu/home.html. 2006 EEA. A. Egger, Ph.D. "The Rock Cycle" Visionlearning Vol. EAS-2 (7), 2005. https://eo.ucar.edu. M. Evans, 2016. 'Water and Carbon Cycling.' https://www.rgs.org/NR/rdonlyres/6FDC37EC-9324-4CE7-8A96-86DFCA1EABB0/0/SCO_WaterandCarbonCycling.pdf [Accessed: 07/2016]. FAO, 2003. 'World agriculture:Towards 2015/2030' http://www.fao.org/docrep/005/y4252e/y4252e06.htm#Ch4 [Accessed: 08/2016]. Kari Greer, National Interagency Fire Center D Hofstrand, 2007. 'Energy Agriculture - Carbon Farming'. http://www.agmrc.org/renewable-energy/climate-change/energy-agriculture-carbon-farming/ [Accessed: 08/2016]. IEA, 2015. 'CO2 Emissions from fuel combustion: IEA statistical highlights' © OECD/IEA, 2015, http://www.iea.org/publications/freepublications/publication/co2-emissions-from-fuel-combustion-highlights-2015.html [Accessed: 08/2016]. M. Ingram, http://apbiomarkip7.blogspot.co.uk [Accessed: 08/2016]. IPCC, 2014. 'Climate Change 2014: Mitigation of Climate Change.' https://www.ipcc.ch/report/ar5/wg3/ [Accessed: 08/2016]. IPCC, 2007. 'IPCC Fourth Assessment Report: Climate Change 2007: Adaptation and mitigation options.' https://www.ipcc.ch/publications_and_data/ar4/syr/en/spms4.html [Accessed: 08/2016]. IPCC. 'Great ocean conveyor belt' http://www.grida.no/climate/ipcc_tar////slides/04.18.htm [Accessed: 08/2016]. IPCC, 2000. 'Land Use, Land-Use Change and Forestry.' http://www.ipcc.ch/ipccreports/sres/land_use/index.php?idp=151#table3-17 [Accessed: 08/2016]. National Snow and Ice Data Center. https://nsidc.org/cryosphere/frozenground/whereis_fg.html [Accessed: 08/2016]. NOAA Ocean Climate Observation Program http://www.oco.noaa.gov/seaSurfaceTempProduct.html [Accessed: 08/2016] NOAA/PMEL. 'Ocean acidification' http://www.pmel.noaa.gov/co2/story/What+is+Ocean+Acidification%3F [Accessed: 08/2016]. Oak Ridge National Laboratory, 2011. "Global Carbon Emissions 2011." Accessed July 6, 2015. http://cdiac.ornl.gov/ftp/ndp030/global.1751_2011.em. [Accessed: 8/2016] © OECD/IEA, 2015. ©OpenGameArt.org. © OpenStax College - Anatomy & Physiology, Connexions Web site, 2013. http://cnx.org/content/col11496/1.6/, Jun 19, 2013., CC BY 3.0, https://commons.wikimedia.org/w/index.php?curid=30131136 [Accessed: 08/2016]. PhysicalGeography.net http://www.physicalgeography.net/fundamentals/8k.html [Accessed: 08/2016]. © 1999-2014 Michael Pidwirny. Rainforest relief.org http://www.rainforestrelief.org/documents/Causes_of_RF_Destruction.gif [Accessed: 08/2016]. REN21, 2016. 'Renewables 2016: Global status report.' http://www.ren21.net/wp-content/uploads/2016/06/GSR_2016_KeyFindings1.pdf [Accessed: 08/2016]. H. Riebeek, NASA Earth Observatory, 2011. 'The carbon cycle.' http://earthobservatory.nasa.gov/Features/CarbonCycle/page1.php [Accessed: 08/2016]. I. Rosa, M. Smith, O. Wearn, D Purves, R. Ewers, 2016. 'The Environmental Legacy of Modern Tropical Deforestation' http://www.cell.com/current-biology/fulltext/S0960-9822(16)30625-X [Accessed: 08/2016]. M. Rubenstein, May 2012. 'Emissions from the Cement Industry.' HTTP://BLOGS.EI.COLUMBIA.EDU/2012/05/09/EMISSIONS-FROM-THE-CEMENT-INDUSTRY/ [Accessed: 08/2016]. © 2016 Salamander Publishing. E. Schuur, J. Bockheim, J. Canadell, E. Euskirchen, C. Field, S. Goryachkin, S. Hagemann, P. Kuhry, P. Lafleur, H. Lee, H, G. Mazhitova, F. Nelson, A. Rinke, V. Romanovsky, N. Shiklomanov, C. Tarnocai, S. Venevsky, J. Vogel, and S. Zimov, Sept 2008. 'Vulnerability of permafrost carbon to climate change: Implications for the global carbon cycle.' BioScience, 58 (8), 701-714.http://bioscience.oxfordjournals.org/content/58/8/701.full.pdf+html [Accessed: 08/2016]. Science Daily https://www.sciencedaily.com/releases/2013/01/130109081141.htm [Accessed: 08/2016]. © 2016 S-cool Youth http://www.s-cool.co.uk/a-level/geography/river-profiles/revise-it/the-water-balance [Accessed 08/2016]. Sepavo via Flickr. P. Sharma, V. Abrol, S. Abrol and R. Kumar, 2012. 'Climate Change and Carbon Sequestration in Dryland Soils, Resource Management for Sustainable Agriculture.' http://www.intechopen.com/books/resource-management-for-sustainable-agriculture/climate-change-and-carbon-sequestration-in-dryland-soils [Accessed: 08/2016]. Shiklomanov and Rodda, 2003. I. Shiklomanov, 1993. "World's fresh water resources" in P. Gleick, 1993. 'Water in Crisis: A Guide to the World's Fresh Water Resources.' http://water.usgs.gov/edu/earthwherewater.html [Accessed: 08/2016]. Warwick Sweeney. UK Ocean Acidification Programme http://www.oceanacidification.org.uk/ [Accessed: 08/2016]. United Nations, Department of Economic and Social Affairs, Population Division, 2014. 'World Urbanization Prospects: The 2014 Revision, Highlights' (ST/ESA/SER.A/352). https://esa.un.org/unpd/wup/Publications/Files/WUP2014-Highlights.pdf [Accessed: 08/2016]. USGS: Hawaiian volcano observatory, 2007 http://hvo.wr.usgs.gov/volcanowatch/archive/2007/07_02_15.html [Accessed: 08/2016]. © Visionlearning, Inc. 2000 – 2016. World Bank, 2014. 'CO2 emissions from transport (% of total fuel combustion)' http://data.worldbank.org/indicator/EN.CO2.TRAN.ZS [Accessed: 08/2016]. World Bank, 2014. 'Understanding CO2 Emissions from the Global Energy Sector.' http://documents.worldbank.org/curated/en/873091468155720710/pdf/851260BRI0Live00Box382147B00PUBLIC0.pdf [Accessed: 08/2016]. World Coal Institute. World Resources Institute (WRI) http://www.wri.org/sites/default/files/WRI13-IPCCinfographic-FINAL_web.png [Accessed: 08/2016]. L. Zhengming and K. Pong. http://www.chinadaily.com.cn/world/2009-06/24/content_8315691.htm [Accessed: 07/2016].

Printed in Germany
by Amazon Distribution
GmbH, Leipzig